Scottish Football Guide and Yearbook

EDITOR
John Robinson

Thirtieth Edition

British Library Cataloguing in Publication Data
A catalogue record for this book is available from the British Library

ISBN: 978-1-86223-524-3

Copyright © 2024, SOCCER BOOKS LIMITED (01472 696226)
72 St. Peter's Avenue, Cleethorpes, DN35 8HU, United Kingdom

Website www.soccer-books.co.uk
e-mail info@soccer-books.co.uk

All rights are reserved. No part of this publication may be reproduced, stored in a retrieval system or transmitted, in any form or by any means, electronic, mechanical, photocopying, recording, or otherwise, without the prior written permission of Soccer Books Limited.

The Publishers, and the Football Clubs itemised are unable to accept liability for any loss, damage or injury caused by error or inaccuracy in the information published in this guide.

Printed in the UK by 4edge Ltd

FOREWORD

We are pleased to say that, following our successful re-launch of our 'Supporters' Guide' series in October 2023, we have been able to produce this fully updated 30th edition in time for the beginning of the 2024-2025 football season. We now show the William Hill Scottish Premiership, the William Hill Scottish Championship, the William Hill Scottish League One and the William Hill Scottish League Two clubs in separate sections within this guide to make it easier to follow for those fans who travel to away matches.

This guide covers The Scottish Professional Football League as well as the Highland Football League and the Scottish Lowland Football League, both of which appear directly below the SPFL in the Scottish pyramid structure. As in previous editions we have included results and final league tables for the 2023-2024 season for the Scottish Professional Football League, Highland Football League and Scottish Lowland Football League.

We wish to thank the club secretaries for their assistance in providing the information contained in this guide. We also wish to thank Bob Budd for the cover artwork.

If readers have up-to-date ground photographs which they wish us to consider for inclusion in a future edition of this guide, please contact us at the address on the title page.

Additional copies of this guide can be obtained directly from us (post free) at the address shown on page 1 overleaf. Alternatively, orders may be placed securely via our website –
www.soccer-books.co.uk
Finally, we would like to wish our readers a safe spectating season.

John Robinson
EDITOR

CONTENTS

Scottish Professional Football League – Premiership Clubs	3-15
Scottish Professional Football League – Championship Clubs	16-26
Scottish Professional Football League – League One Clubs	27-37
Scottish Professional Football League – League Two Clubs	38-48
Highland Football League Clubs	49-67
Scottish Lowland Football League Clubs	68-86
Statistics – Results and Final Tables – 2023-2024 Season	87-92
2023-2024 Scottish Cup Results	93-95
2023-2024 Scottish League Cup Results	96-98
2023-2024 Scottish League Challenge Cup Results	99-100
2023-2024 Scotland Internationals	101-103

THE SCOTTISH PROFESSIONAL FOOTBALL LEAGUE

WILLIAM HILL SCOTTISH PREMIERSHIP

Address
National Stadium, Hampden Park,
Mount Florida, Glasgow G42 9DE

Website www.spfl.co.uk
E-mail info@spfl.co.uk Phone (0141) 620-4140

Clubs for the 2024-2025 Season

Aberdeen FC .... Page 4

Celtic FC .... Page 5

Dundee FC .... Page 6

Dundee United FC .... Page 7

Heart of Midlothian FC .... Page 8

Hibernian FC .... Page 9

Kilmarnock FC .... Page 10

Motherwell FC .... Page 11

Rangers FC .... Page 12

Ross County FC .... Page 13

St. Johnstone FC .... Page 14

St. Mirren FC .... Page 15

ABERDEEN FC

Founded: 1903 (**Entered League:** 1904)
Nickname: 'The Reds' 'The Dons' 'The Dandies'
Ground: Pittodrie Stadium, Pittodrie Street, Aberdeen AB24 5QH
Ground Capacity: 20,866 (all seats)
Record Attendance: 45,061 (13th March 1954)

Colours: Red shirts and shorts
Telephone Nº: (01224) 650400
Ticket Office: (01224) 631903
Website: www.afc.co.uk
E-mail: contact@afc.co.uk

GENERAL INFORMATION
Car Parking: Beach Promenade, King Street and Golf Road
Coach Parking: At the rear of the Stadium in Golf Road car park (£10.00 charge)
Nearest Railway Station: Aberdeen (1 mile)
Nearest Bus Station: Aberdeen
Club Shop: At the ground
Opening Times: Monday to Friday 9.30am to 5.30pm and Saturday 9.30am to 5.00pm.
Telephone Nº: (01224) 642800

GROUND INFORMATION
Away Supporters' Entrances & Sections:
Park Road entrance for the South Stand East

ADMISSION INFO (2024/2025 PRICES)
Adults: £22.00 – £32.00
Over-65s: £20.00 – £25.00
Youths & Over-75s: £16.00 – £20.00
Under-18s: £12.00 – £15.00
Under-12s: £6.00 – £12.00

DISABLED INFORMATION
Wheelchairs: 7 spaces available in the South Stand for away fans. 26 spaces in total for home fans
Helpers: One helper admitted per wheelchair
Prices: Concessionary prices for fans with disabilities requiring assistance. Free of charge for helpers.
Disabled Toilets: Available in the Richard Donald Stand, the Merkland Stand, in the Away Section and in a new toilet block at the Richard Donald Stand entrance
Contact: (01224) 631903 (Bookings are necessary) –

Travelling Supporters' Information:
Routes: From the City Centre, travel along Union Street then turn left into King Street. The Stadium is about ½ mile along King Street (A92) on the right-hand side.

CELTIC FC

Founded: 1888 (**Entered League**: 1890)
Nickname: 'The Bhoys' 'The Hoops'
Ground: Celtic Park, Glasgow G40 3RE
Ground Capacity: 60,411 (All seats)
Record Attendance: 83,500 (1st January 1938)

Colours: Green & White hooped shirts, White shorts
General Telephone Nº: 0871 226-1888
Ticket Office E-mail: tickets@celticfc.co.uk
Website: www.celticfc.net

GENERAL INFORMATION

Car Parking: Limited on Matchdays to those with a Valid Car Park Pass. Otherwise, street parking
Coach Parking: Gallowgate, Fielden Street, Biggar Street and Nuneaton Street
Nearest Railway Station: Bellgrove (10 minutes walk)
Nearest Bus Stop: Outside of the ground
Club Shop: Superstore at Celtic Park. Also in Glasgow: 154 Argyle Street and Terminal Building, Glasgow Airport. Elsewhere: Unit 26, Princes Square, East Kilbride Shopping Centre; 99 Sylvania Way, Clyde Shopping Centre, Clydebank; 72 Main Street, Coatbridge; Unit 6, The Centre, Almondvale Boulevard, Livingston; at Braehead Shopping Centre; 30/34 Ann Street, Belfast; 125 Upper Abbey Street, Dublin.
Opening Times: Please check www.celticfc.net for details
Telephone Nº: (0141) 551-4231 (Superstore)

GROUND INFORMATION

Away Supporters' Entrances & Sections:
Kinloch Street Turnstiles for the East (Lisbon Lions) Stand

ADMISSION INFO (2024/2025 PRICES)

Please contact the club for information about ticket pricing during the 2024/2025 season.
Note: Most of the seats are taken by season ticket holders

DISABLED INFORMATION

Wheelchairs: 141 spaces for home fans and 6 spaces for away fans in the North Stand and East Stand
Prices: Normal prices apply for disabled fans. Helpers are admitted free of charge.
Disabled Toilets: 23 accessible toilets throughout the Park and a special Changing Place toilet in the North Stand.
Contact: (0141) 551-4373 (Bookings are necessary) – Disability Officer Alexis Dobbin: alexis.dobbin@celticfc.co.uk

Travelling Supporters' Information:
Routes: From the South and East: Take the A74 London Road towards the City Centre, Celtic Park is on the right about ½ mile past the Belvidere Hospital and the ground is clearly visible; From the West: Take the A74 London Road from the City Centre and turn left about ½ mile past Bridgeton Station.

DUNDEE FC

Founded: 1893 (**Entered League**: 1893)
Nickname: 'The Dee'
Ground: The Scot Foam Stadium, Dens Park, Sandeman Street, Dundee DD3 7JY
Ground Capacity: 11,850 (All seats)
Record Attendance: 43,024 (7th February 1953)

Colours: Shirts are Blue with White sleeves, White shorts
Telephone Nº: (01382) 889966 (option 1)
Ticket Office: (01382) 767039
Website: www.dundeefc.co.uk
E-mail: reception@dundeefc.co.uk

GENERAL INFORMATION
Car Parking: Street parking only
Coach Parking: Please contact the club for details
Nearest Railway Station: Dundee
Nearest Bus Station: Dundee
Club Shop: At the Stadium
Opening Times: Weekdays from 10.00am to 5.00pm and Saturday 10.00am to 3.00pm.
Telephone Nº: (01382) 889966

GROUND INFORMATION
Away Supporters' Entrances & Sections:
Turnstiles 33-38 for Bob Shankley Stand accommodation

ADMISSION INFO (2024/2025 PRICES)
Adult Seating: £26.00 – £32.00
Under-12s Seating: £4.00 – £6.00
Concessionary Seating: £16.00 – £20.00
Please contact the club for further admission information.

DISABLED INFORMATION
Wheelchairs: Accommodated in the East and West Stands
Helpers: Admitted free of charge
Prices: Concessionary prices apply
Disabled Toilets: Adjacent to the Disabled Area
Contact: (01382) 889966 (Bookings are necessary) – John Burke (Disability Officer): slo@dundeefc.co.uk

Travelling Supporters' Information:
Routes: Take the A972 from Perth (Kingsway West) to King's Cross Circus Roundabout. Take the 3rd exit into Clepington Road and turn right into Provost Road for 1 mile then take the 2nd left into Sandeman Street for the ground.

DUNDEE UNITED FC

Founded: 1909 (**Entered League**: 1910)
Former Names: Dundee Hibernians FC
Nickname: 'The Terrors'
Ground: Calforth Construction Arena at Tannadice Park, Tannadice Street, Dundee DD3 7JW
Ground Capacity: 14,223 (all seats)
Record Attendance: 28,000 (November 1966)

Colours: Tangerine shirts with Black shorts
Telephone Nº: (01382) 833166
Ticket Office: (01382) 833166 Option 1
Website: www.dundeeunitedfc.co.uk
E-mail: admin@dundeeunitedfc.co.uk

GENERAL INFORMATION
Car Parking: Street Parking only
Coach Parking: GA Arena (home coaches)
Nearest Railway Station: Dundee (20 minutes walk)
Nearest Bus Station: Dundee
Club Shop: In Tannadice Street
Opening Times: Weekdays 9.00am–5.00pm (Thursday 6pm) Saturday (away matches) 9.00am–1.00pm. Saturday/Sunday matchdays 9.00am to kick-off then 30 minutes after the game.
Telephone Nº: (01382) 833166 (option 3)

GROUND INFORMATION
Away Supporters' Entrances & Sections:
Turnstiles 7-16 for Jerry Kerr Stand & Jim McLean Fair Play Stand

ADMISSION INFO (2024/2025 PRICES)
Adult Seating: £31.00 – £34.00
Concessionary Seating: £17.00 – £20.00
Under-12s Seating: £10.00 (with a paying adult)

DISABLED INFORMATION
Wheelchairs: Accommodated in the George Fox Stand, the Eddie Thompson Stand and Jim McLean Fair Play Stand (away).
Prices: Concessionary prices for disabled fans, helpers free
Disabled Toilets: Available in the George Fox Stand, the Eddie Thompson Stand and Jim McLean Fair Play Stand.
Contact: (01382) 833166 Option 1 (Bookings necessary) Moira Hughes (Disability Officer): moira@dundeeunitedfc.co.uk

Travelling Supporters' Information:
Routes: From the South or West: Travel via Perth and take the A90 to Dundee. Once in Dundee join the Kingsway (ring road) and follow until the third exit marked "Football Traffic", then turn right onto Old Glamis Road. Follow the road to join Provost Road then turn left into Sandeman Street for the ground; From the North: Follow the A90 from Aberdeen and join the Kingsway (ring road). At the first set of traffic lights turn right into Clepington Road and follow into Arklay Street before turning right into Tannadice Street for the ground.

HEART OF MIDLOTHIAN FC

Founded: 1874 (**Entered League**: 1890)
Nickname: 'The Jam Tarts' 'Jambos'
Ground: Tynecastle Park, McLeod Street, Edinburgh EH11 2NL
Ground Capacity: 20,099 (All seats)
Record Attendance: 53,396 (13th January 1932)

Colours: Maroon shirts with White shorts
Telephone Nº: 0333 043-1874
Ticket Office Nº: 0333 043-1874 (Option 1)
Website: www.heartsfc.co.uk

GENERAL INFORMATION
Car Parking: Street Parking in Robertson Avenue and Wheatfield Road but none available at the ground itself
Coach Parking: Russell Road
Nearest Railway Station: Edinburgh Haymarket (½ mile)
Nearest Bus Station: St. Andrew's Square
Club Store: At the ground
Opening Times: Thursday to Saturday Matchdays 10.00am to 6.00pm
Telephone Nº: 0333 043-1874

GROUND INFORMATION
Away Supporters' Entrances & Sections: Roseburn Stand entrances and accommodation

ADMISSION INFO (2024/2025 PRICES)
Adult Seating: £20.00 – £36.00
Senior Citizen/Student Seating: £15.00 – £29.00
Under-18s Seating: £12.00 – £21.00
Under-13s Seating: £5.00 – £16.00
Note: Prices vary depending on the category of the game but very few seats will be available for most home games

DISABLED INFORMATION
Wheelchairs: 92 spaces available for home and away fans in Wheatfield, Roseburn & Gorgie Stands
Prices: Concessionary prices for wheelchair users and the blind/partially sighted. Helpers admitted free of charge.
Disabled Toilets: Available
Contact: 0333 043-1874 (Bookings are necessary)
Keith Ferguson (Disability Officer): 07719032111

Travelling Supporters' Information:
Routes: From the West: Take the A71 (Ayr Road) into Gorgie Road and the ground is about ¾ mile past Saughton Park on the left; From the North: Take the A90 Queensferry Road and turn right into Drum Brae after about ½ mile. Follow Drum Brae into Meadowplace Road (about 1 mile) then Broomhouse Road to the junction with Calder Road. Turn right, then as from the West; From the South: Take the A702/A703 to the A720 (Oxgangs Road). Turn left and follow the A720 into Wester Hailes Road (2½ miles) until the junction with Calder Road. Turn right, then as from the West.

HIBERNIAN FC

Founded: 1875 (**Entered League**: 1893)
Nickname: 'The Hi-Bees'
Ground: Easter Road Stadium, 12 Albion Place, Edinburgh EH7 5QG
Ground Capacity: 20,421 (all seats)
Record Attendance: 65,860 (2nd January 1950)

Colours: Green and White shirts with White shorts
Telephone Nº: (0131) 661-2159
Ticket Office: (0131) 661-2159 Option 2
Website: www.hibernianfc.co.uk
E-mail: club@hibernianfc.co.uk

GENERAL INFORMATION
Car Parking: Street parking
Coach Parking: Regent Road (by Police Direction)
Nearest Railway Station: Edinburgh Waverley (25 minutes walk)
Nearest Bus Station: St. Andrews Square
Club Shop: In the Famous Five Stand at the ground
Opening Times: Monday to Saturday 10.00am – 5.00pm,
Club Shop e-mail: info@hiberniandirect.co.uk
Telephone Nº: (0131) 656-7078

GROUND INFORMATION
Away Supporters' Entrances & Sections:
South Stand entrances and accommodation

ADMISSION INFO (2024/2025 PRICES)
Adult Seating: £24.00 – £36.00
Concessionary Seating: £14.00 – £22.00
Child Seating: £10.00 – £14.00
Note: Prices depend on category of game.

DISABLED INFORMATION
Wheelchairs: 14 spaces in the West Stand, 16 spaces in the East Stand, 11 spaces in the Famous Five Stand + 11 spaces in the South Stand. Also, 46 dual spaces in both the South Stand and Famous Five Stand
Helpers: One helper admitted per disabled person
Prices: Normal prices for the disabled. Free for helpers
Disabled Toilets: 4 available in the Famous Five and South Stands, 5 in the West Stand and 2 in the East Stand
Contact: (0131) 656-7066
(Bookings are necessary for home supporters only – away Supporters should book and pay through their own club)
Joyce Harvie (Disability Officer):
accessibletickets@hibernianfc.co.uk

Travelling Supporters' Information:
Routes: From the West and North: Take the A90 Queensferry Road to the A902 and continue for 2¼ miles. Turn right into Great Junction Street and follow into Duke Street then Lochend Road. Turn sharp right into Hawkhill Avenue at Lochend Park and follow the road into Albion Place for the ground; From the South: Take the A1 through Musselburgh (Milton Road/Willow Brae/London Road) and turn right into Easter Road after about 2½ miles. Take the 4th right into Albion Road for the ground.

KILMARNOCK FC

Founded: 1869 (**Entered League**: 1896)
Nickname: 'Killie'
Ground: The BBSP Stadium, Rugby Park, Rugby Road, Kilmarnock, Ayrshire KA1 2DP (SatNav use the following postcode: KA1 1UR)
Record Attendance: 35,995 (10th March 1962)

Ground Capacity: 18,128 (all seats)
Colours: Blue & White striped shirts, Blue shorts
Telephone Nº: (01563) 545300
Ticket Office Nº: (01563) 545311
Website: www.kilmarnockfc.co.uk
E-mail: info@kilmarnockfc.co.uk

GENERAL INFORMATION
Car Parking: At the ground (Permit Holders only). Otherwise, street parking.
Coach Parking: Fairyhill Road Bus Park
Nearest Railway Station: Kilmarnock (15 minutes walk)
Nearest Bus Station: Kilmarnock (10 minutes walk)
Club Shop: Killie Shop, adjacent to the West Stand
Opening Times: Monday to Friday 9.00am – 5.00pm, Saturdays 10.00am – 4.00pm (until kick-off on matchdays).
Telephone Nº: (01563) 545310
E-mail: killieshop@kilmarnockfc.co.uk

GROUND INFORMATION
Away Supporters' Entrances & Sections:
Rugby Road turnstiles for the Chadwick Stand

ADMISSION INFO (2024/2025 PRICES)
Adult Seating: £30.00 – £33.00
Concessionary Seating: £25.00 – £28.00
Under-16s Seating: £12.00 – £16.00
Note: Prices vary for Old Firm and Cup games.

DISABLED INFORMATION
Wheelchairs: 15 spaces each for home and away fans in the Main Stand
Helpers: One helper admitted per wheelchair
Prices: Prices vary depending on reciprocal arrangements
Disabled Toilets: 2 available in the Chadwick Stand and Moffat Stand, access via the Radar Key system.
Contact: Kilmarnock FC Disabled Supporters' Association on (01563) 537522 or 07759 616945 (Peter Orr, Disability Officer)

Travelling Supporters' Information:
Routes: From Glasgow/Ayr: Take the A77 Kilmarnock Bypass. Exit at the Bellfield Interchange. Take the A71 (Irvine) to the first roundabout then take the A759 (Kilmarnock Town Centre). The ground is ½ mile on the left hand side.

MOTHERWELL FC

Founded: 1886 (**Entered League**: 1893)
Nickname: 'The Steelmen'
Ground: Fir Park, Fir Park Street, Motherwell, ML1 2QN
Ground Capacity: 13,677 (all seats)
Record Attendance: 35,632 (12th March 1952)
Colours: Shirts are Amber with a Claret chestband and Claret trim, Shorts are Amber with Claret trim
Telephone/Ticket Office N°: (01698) 333333
Website: www.motherwellfc.co.uk
E-mail: mfcenquiries@motherwellfc.co.uk

GENERAL INFORMATION
Car Parking: Street parking and nearby Car Parks
Coach Parking: Orbiston Street
Nearest Railway Station: Airbles (1 mile)
Nearest Bus Station: Motherwell
Club Shop: At the ground
Opening Times: Monday to Saturday 9.30am to 5.00pm (until 1.00pm on away match Saturdays)
Telephone N°: (01698) 338025

GROUND INFORMATION
Away Supporters' Entrances & Sections:
Dalziel Drive entrances for the South Stand

ADMISSION INFO (2024/2025 PRICES)
Adult Seating: £24.00 – £33.00
Concessionary Seating: £19.00 – £24.00
Ages 12 to 17 Seating: £12.00
Under-12s Seating: £6.00
Note: Discounts are available in the Family Section and prices vary depending on the category of the game

DISABLED INFORMATION
Wheelchairs: 20 spaces for home fans and 10 spaces for away fans in the Phil O'Donnell Main Stand and South Stand
Helpers: Admitted
Prices: Concessionary prices are charged for disabled fans
Disabled Toilets: Available in all disabled areas
Contact: thomsalex94@gmail.com
e-mail: tickets@mfcdsa.com (Must book 1 week in advance)

Travelling Supporters' Information:
Routes: From the East: Take the A723 into Merry Street and turn left into Brandon Street (1 mile). Follow through to Windmill Hill Street and turn right at the Fire Station into Knowetop Avenue for the ground; From Elsewhere: Exit the M74 at Junction 4 and take the A723 Hamilton Road into the Town Centre. Turn right into West Hamilton Street and follow into Brandon Street – then as from the East.

RANGERS FC

Founded: 1872 (**Entered League**: 1890)
Nickname: 'The Gers' 'Light Blues'
Ground: Ibrox Stadium, 150 Edmiston Drive, Glasgow G51 2XD
Ground Capacity: 50,817 (All seats)
Record Attendance: 118,567 (2nd January 1939)

Colours: Shirts are Blue with White trim around the collar, White shorts
Telephone N°: 0871 702-1972 (13p per minute)
Ticket Office: 0871 702-1972 Option 1
Website: www.rangers.co.uk
E-mail: ticketcentre@rangers.co.uk

GENERAL INFORMATION
Car Parking: Albion Car Park (£10.00 charge)
Coach Parking: By Police direction
Away fans Car/Coach Parking: Broomloan Road
Nearest Underground Station: Ibrox (2 minutes walk)
Nearest Bus Station: Glasgow City Centre
Club Shop: Rangers Megastore, Ibrox Stadium
Opening Times: Monday to Friday 9.30am to 5.30pm, Saturdays 9.00am – 5.30pm and Sundays 11.00am – 5.00pm. Opening hours may vary depending on match times
Megastore Telephone N°: (0141) 427-4444

GROUND INFORMATION
Away Supporters' Entrances & Sections:
Govan West Corner and turnstiles

ADMISSION INFO (2024/2025 PRICES)
Please contact the club for information about ticket pricing during the 2024/2025 season.
Note: Most of the seats are taken by season ticket holders

DISABLED INFORMATION
Wheelchairs: 68 spaces for home fans in front of the West Enclosure, 35 spaces in front of the East Enclosure, 4 spaces in the Broomloan Stand and 7 spaces for away fans in the Govan West Stand Corner
Helpers: Admitted
Prices: Most disabled spaces are allocated to season ticket holders and are priced in accordance with the general prices.
Disabled Toilets: Available throughout the stadium
Contact: (0141)580-8778 (Bookings required)
John Spain (Disability Officer):
disabilitymatters@rangers.co.uk

Travelling Supporters' Information:
Routes: As the M8, travelling west from the Kingston Bridge, no longer allows traffic to exit at Junction 23, traffic must now exit at either Junction 24 (Helen Street) or Junction 25 (Cardonald). Access to Ibrox is then eastwards along Edmiston Drive/Shieldhall Road. Drivers of westbound vehicles travelling to Ibrox for home games are encouraged to exit the M74 at Tradeston where they can either travel onto the M77 and come off at Junction 1 (Dumbreck Road) or turn right onto Carnoustie Street and left onto Paisley Road and head to Ibrox Stadium from there.

ROSS COUNTY FC

Founded: 1929 (**Entered League**: 1994)
Nickname: 'The Staggies'
Ground: GLobal Energy Stadium, Victoria Park, Jubilee Park Road, Dingwall   IV15 9QZ
Ground Capacity: 6,541 (All seats)
Record Attendance: 8,500 (vs Rangers in 1966)

Colours: Navy Blue shirts and shorts
Telephone Nº: (01349) 860860
Ticket Office: (01349) 860860
Website: www.rosscountyfootballclub.co.uk
E-mail: info@rosscountyfootballclub.co.uk

GENERAL INFORMATION
Car Parking: At the ground (£3.00 charge)
Coach Parking: At the ground
Nearest Railway Station: Dingwall (adjacent)
Nearest Bus Station: Dingwall
Club Shop: At the ground, outside the West Stand
Opening Times: Monday to Thursday 10.00am to 4.00pm, Friday 10.00am to 3.00pm and Saturday Matchdays from 10.00am.
Telephone Nº: (01349) 860860

GROUND INFORMATION
Away Supporters' Entrances & Sections:
North Stand entrances and accommodation

ADMISSION INFO (2024/2025 PRICES)
Adult Seating: £28.00
Concessionary Seating: £15.00
Under-18s Seating: £10.00
Under-12s Seating: £6.00

DISABLED INFORMATION
Wheelchairs: 6 spaces each for home and away fans
Helpers: Admitted
Prices: Concessionary prices for the disabled. Helpers free
Disabled Toilets: Available at the bottom of the West Stand
Contact: (01349) 860860   (Bookings are necessary) David O'Connor – Disability Officer:
E-mail: david.oconnor@rosscountyfootballclub.co.uk

Travelling Supporters' Information:
Routes: The ground is situated at Dingwall adjacent to the Railway Station which is down Jubilee Park Road at the bottom of the High Street.

ST. JOHNSTONE FC

Founded: 1884 (**Entered League**: 1911)
Nickname: 'Saints'
Ground: McDiarmid Park, Crieff Road, Perth, PH1 2SJ
Ground Capacity: 10,696 (All seats)
Record Attendance: 10,545 (vs Dundee, 23/5/1999)
Colours: Blue shirts with White shorts
Telephone Nº: (01738) 459090
Ticket Office: (01738) 455000
Website: www.perthstjohnstonefc.co.uk
E-mail: enquiries@perthsaints.co.uk

GENERAL INFORMATION
Car Parking: Car park at the ground (£5.00 charge)
Coach Parking: At the ground
Nearest Railway Station: Perth (3 miles)
Nearest Bus Station: Perth (3 miles)
Club Shop: At the ground
Opening Times: Weekdays from 9.00am to 5.00pm and Matchdays 1.30pm to 3.00pm
Telephone Nº: (01738) 459090

GROUND INFORMATION
Away Supporters' Entrances & Sections:
North Stand and/or the North End of the West Stand and/or the South Stand.

ADMISSION INFO (2024/2025 PRICES)
Adult Seating: £26.00
Under-20s Seating: £16.00
Senior Citizens: £16.00
Note: Under-12s are admitted free of charge when accompanied by a paying adult (up to two per adult)

DISABLED INFORMATION
Wheelchairs: 8 spaces available for home fans in both the East and West Stands. 8 spaces for away fans in the West Stand.
Prices: For disabled fans: £15.00 for Adults and £9.00 for Senior Citizens/Under-16s. Helpers admitted free of charge
Disabled Toilets: Available in the East and West Stands
Contact: (01738) 459090 (Bookings are preferable) – Beverley Mayer (Disability Officer): dao@perthsaints.co.uk

Travelling Supporters' Information:
Routes: Follow the M80 to Stirling, take the A9 Inverness Road north from Perth and follow the signs for the 'Football Stadium'. The ground is situated beside a dual-carriageway – the Perth Western By-pass near Junction 11 of the M90.

ST. MIRREN FC

Founded: 1877 (**Entered League**: 1890)
Nickname: 'The Saints' 'The Buddies'
Ground: The SMiSA Stadium, St. Mirren Park, Greenhill Road, Paisley   PA3 1RU
Ground Capacity: 8,023 (all seats)
Record Attendance: 47,438 (vs Celtic in 1949 – at the old stadium in Love Street)

Colours: Black and White striped shirts, Black shorts
Telephone Nº: (0141) 889-2558
Ticket Line Nº: (0141) 840-6120
Main Website: www.stmirren.com
Ticketing Website: www.smfctickets.co.uk
E-mail: info@stmirren.com

GENERAL INFORMATION

Car Parking: Street parking plus limited parking in the Stadium car park (£5.00 charge)
Coach Parking: Clark Street
Nearest Railway Station: Paisley St. James (400 yards) or Paisley Gilmour Street (10 minutes walk)
Nearest Bus Station: Paisley
Club Shop: At the stadium
Opening Times: Weekdays only 9.30am to 4.00pm
Telephone Nº: (0141) 840-6130

GROUND INFORMATION
Away Supporters' Entrances & Sections:
North Stand (N1-N5), turnstiles 17-20

ADMISSION INFO (2024/2025 PRICES)
Adult Seating: £22.00 – £27.00
Concessionary Seating: £12.00 – £17.00
Under-18s Seating: £12.00 – £17.00
Under-12s Seating: £6.00 – £17.00

DISABLED INFORMATION
Wheelchairs: Accommodated in all Stands
Helpers: Admitted
Prices: Concessionary prices for the disabled. Helpers are admitted free of charge.
Disabled Toilets: Available in all the stands
Contact: (0141) 840-6130   (Bookings are necessary)
John White or John Allison Email: slo@stmirren.com

Travelling Supporters' Information:
Routes: From All Parts: Exit the M8 at Junction 29 and take the A726, keeping in the middle lane to avoid the A727 which is signposted for Irvine. At the St. James interchange, turn left onto the dual carriageway (Greenock Road) which has football pitches on the left. After the sharp bend, take the first turn on the right into Clark Street and, at the T-junction, turn left past the railway station into Greenhill Road. The stadium is on the right-hand side of the road.

THE SCOTTISH PROFESSIONAL FOOTBALL LEAGUE

WILLIAM HILL SCOTTISH CHAMPIONSHIP

Address
National Stadium, Hampden Park,
Mount Florida, Glasgow   G42 9DE

Website   www.spfl.co.uk
E-mail   info@spfl.co.uk
Phone   (0141) 620-4140

Clubs for the 2024-2025 Season

Airdrieonians FC .... Page 17
Ayr United FC .... Page 18
Dunfermline Athletic FC... Page 19
Greenock Morton FC .... Page 20
Hamilton Academical FC .... Page 21
Inverness Caledonian Thistle FC .... Page 22
Livingston FC.. Page 23
Partick Thistle FC .... Page 24
Queen's Park FC .... Page 25
Raith Rovers FC .... Page 26

AIRDRIEONIANS FC

Founded: 1965 (**Entered League**: 1966)
Former Name: Clydebank FC and Airdrie United FC
Ground: The Albert Bartlett Stadium, Craigneuk Avenue, Airdrie   ML6 8QZ
Ground Capacity: 9,843 (All seats)
Record Attendance: 9,044 (vs Rangers, 23/8/2013)

Colours: White shirts with Red diamond, White shorts
Telephone Nº: (01236) 803778
Ticket Office: 07710 2307720
Website: www.airdriefc.com
E-mail: Contact via a form on the club's website

GENERAL INFORMATION
Car Parking: Behind all the Stands
Coach Parking: Behind the East Stand
Nearest Railway Station: Drumgelloch (½ mile)
Nearest Bus Station: Gartlea – Airdrie Town Centre
Club Shop: At the ground
Opening Times: Opens at 12.00pm on Home Matchdays and Sunday 2.00pm – 4.00pm
Telephone Nº: (01236) 803778

GROUND INFORMATION
Away Supporters' Entrances & Sections:
The Jack Dalziel Stand and the Osprey Global East Stand

ADMISSION INFO (2024/2025 PRICES)
Adult Seating: £22.00
Under-16s Seating: £9.00
Concessionary Seating: £14.00 – £17.00
Note: Parent and Child tickets are priced at £27.00

DISABLED INFORMATION
Wheelchairs: Spaces available for home and away fans accommodated in the front sections
Helpers: One admitted per disabled supporter
Prices: Concessionary prices for disabled fans with helpers admitted free of charge.
Disabled Toilets: Available in all the stands
Contact: (01236) 803778   (Bookings are preferable) – slo@airdrieonians.co.uk

Travelling Supporters' Information:
Routes: From the East: Exit the M8 at Junction 6 and take the A73 (signposted for Cumbernauld). Pass through Chapelhall into Airdrie and turn right into Petersburn Road – the ground is on the left; From the West: Take the A8 to the Chapelhall turn-off for Chapelhall. Join the A73 at Chapelhall, then as above.

AYR UNITED FC

Founded: 1910 (**Entered League**: 1910)
Former Names: Formed by the amagamation of Ayr Parkhouse FC and Ayr FC in 1910
Nickname: 'The Honest Men'
Ground: Somerset Park, Tryfield Place, Ayr, KA8 9NB
Ground Capacity: 10,185
Seating Capacity: 1,597

Record Attendance: 25,225 (13th September 1969)
Colours: Black and White shirts with Black shorts
Telephone/Ticket Office N°: (01292) 263435
Website: www.ayrunitedfc.co.uk
E-mail: tracy@ayrunitedfc.co.uk

GENERAL INFORMATION
Car Parking: Craigie Car Park, Ayr Racecourse and Somerset Road Car Park
Coach Parking: Craigie Car Park
Nearest Railway Station: Ayr or Newton-on-Ayr (both stations are 10 minutes walk)
Nearest Bus Station: Sandgate, Ayr
Club Shop: At the ground
Opening Times: Monday, Wednesday, Thursday and Friday 1.00pm to 5.00pm plus Matchdays from 11.00am to kick-off
Telephone N°: (01292) 263435

GROUND INFORMATION
Away Supporters' Entrances & Sections:
Railway End Terrace use gates 2, 3 and 5; West Enclosure and West Stand use gates 9 and 10

ADMISSION INFO (2024/2025 PRICES)
Adult Standing/Seating: £22.00
Student/Senior Citizen Standing/Seating: £15.00
Ages 13 to 17 Standing/Seating: £15.00
Children (Under-13s) Standing/Seating: £6.00

DISABLED INFORMATION
Wheelchairs: 24 spaces are available in the Disabled Area beneath the Family Stand
Helpers: One admitted per wheelchair
Prices: Concessionary prices for disabled fans. Helpers are admitted free of charge
Disabled Toilets: Available in the Disabled Area
Are Bookings Necessary: Only for all-ticket games
Contact: (01292) 263435 Roy Provan (Disability Officer) – stadium@ayrunitedfc.co.uk

Travelling Supporters' Information:
Routes: Make for the A77 Ring Road around Ayr, exit via Whitletts Roundabout onto the A719 and follow the road towards Ayr. Just past the end of the racecourse, turn right at the traffic lights into Burnett Terrace, a sharp left and then right takes you into Somerset Road for the ground. (For car parking on Matchdays turn left at the traffic lights and then right 50 yards on into Craigie Park or on Somerset Road just past the ground on the left into Somerset Road car park).

DUNFERMLINE ATHLETIC FC

Founded: 1885 (**Entered League**: 1921)
Nickname: 'The Pars'
Ground: KDM East End Park, Halbeath Road, Dunfermline, Fife KY12 7RB
Ground Capacity: 11,480 (All seats)
Record Attendance: 27,816 (30th April 1968)

Colours: Black and White Striped shirts, Black shorts
Telephone Nº: (01383) 724295
Ticket Office: (01383) 745909
Website: www.dafc.co.uk
E-mail: enquiries@dafc.co.uk

GENERAL INFORMATION

Car Parking: Limited spaces in a Car Park at the ground.
Coach Parking: Leys Park Road
Nearest Railway Station: Dunfermline Queen Margaret (10 minutes walk)
Nearest Bus Station: Queen Anne Street, Dunfermline (10 minutes walk)
Club Shop: At the Ground
Opening Times: Friday 10.00am – 4.00pm, Saturday 10.00am to 12.00pm and Saturday Matchdays 10.00am–3.00pm then 5.00pm–5.30pm
Telephone Nº: (01383) 724295

GROUND INFORMATION

Away Supporters' Entrances & Sections: Turnstiles 10-15 for the East Stand. Turnstiles 16-18 for the North East Stand

ADMISSION INFO (2024/2025 PRICES)

Adult Seating: £21.00 – £23.00
Under-18s/Other Concessions Seating: £15.00 – £17.00
Under-12s Seating: £7.00 – £9.00

DISABLED INFORMATION

Wheelchairs: 19 spaces for home, 12 spaces for away fans
Helpers: One admitted per wheelchair
Prices: Concessionary prices for the wheelchair disabled. Helpers are admitted free of charge
Disabled Toilets: Available in West and East Stands and also in the Main Stand Hospitality Area
Contact: (01383) 745909 (Bookings are necessary – E-mail dao@dafc.co.uk – Graham Ross 07877980028

Travelling Supporters' Information:
Routes: From the Forth Road Bridge and Perth: Exit the M90 at Junction 3 and take the A907 (Halbeath Road) into Dunfermline – the ground is on right; From Kincardine Bridge and Alloa: Take the A985 to the A994 into Dunfermline. Take Pittencrieff Street, Glen Bridge and Carnegie Drive to Sinclair Gardens roundabout. Take the 1st exit toward the Traffic Lights then turn right into Ley's Park Road. Take the second exit on the right into the Car Park at the rear of the stadium.

FALKIRK FC

Founded: 1876 (**Entered League**: 1902)
Nickname: 'The Bairns'
Ground: The Falkirk Stadium, 4 Stadium Way, Falkirk FK2 9EE
Ground Capacity: 7,937 (All seats)

Colours: Navy Blue shirts with White shorts
Telephone N°: (01324) 624121
Ticket Office: (01324) 624121
Website: www.falkirkfc.co.uk
E-mail: enquiries@falkirkfc.co.uk

GENERAL INFORMATION
Car Parking: A large Car Park is adjacent
Coach Parking: Available at the rear of the North Stand
Nearest Railway Station: Falkirk Grahamston (1 mile)
Nearest Bus Station: Falkirk (1 mile)
Club Shop: At the stadium
Opening Times: Weekdays 10.00am to 2.00pm
Telephone N°: (01324) 624121 (Option 1)

GROUND INFORMATION
Away Supporters' Entrances & Sections:
North Stand

ADMISSION INFO (2024/2025 PRICES)
Adult Seating: £20.00 – £23.00
Under-18s Seating: £10.00 – £13.00 (Under-12s free)
Concessionary Seating: £15.00 – £18.00
Note: Family Tickets are also available
Please contact the club for further admission information

DISABLED INFORMATION
Wheelchairs: Accommodated in the North, South and West Stands
Helpers: Admitted
Prices: Free of charge for both disabled fans and helpers
Disabled Toilets: Available
Contact: (01324) 624121 (Bookings are necessary) – Kenny McDonald (Disability Officer): dao@falkirkfc.co.uk

Travelling Supporters' Information:
Routes: Exit the M9 at Junction 6 and take the A904 towards Falkirk. Continue into Falkirk at the Westfield/Laurieston roundabout along Grangemouth Road and take the first right into Alexander Avenue. Then take the 2nd right into Westfield Street and the ground is on the right.

GREENOCK MORTON FC

Founded: 1874 (**Entered League**: 1893)
Nickname: 'Ton'
Ground: Cappielow Park, Sinclair Street, Greenock, PA15 2TU
Ground Capacity: 11,589
Seating Capacity: 5,741

Record Attendance: 23,500 (v Celtic, 29/4/1921)
Colours: Blue and White hooped shirts, White shorts
Telephone/Ticket Office N°: (01475) 723571
Website: www.gmfc.net
E-mail: admin@gmfc.net

GENERAL INFORMATION
Car Parking: At the ground (£3.00 fee) or Street parking
Coach Parking: James Watt Dock
Nearest Railway Station: Cartsdyke (½ mile)
Nearest Bus Station: Town Centre (1½ miles)
Club Shop: Within "Smiths of Greenock", West Blackhall Street, Greenock. There is also a Merchandise Unit in Sinclair Street, outside of the ground open matchdays only.
Opening Times: Monday to Saturday 9.00am to 5.30pm
Telephone N°: (01475) 888555
Club Shop Website: www.smithsofgreenock.co.uk

GROUND INFORMATION
Away Supporters' Entrances & Sections:
In the Grandstand

ADMISSION INFO (2024/2025 PRICES)
Adult Standing and Seating: £22.00
Concessionary Standing/Seating: £16.00
Under-16s Standing/Seating: £5.00
Note: Under-12s must be accompanied by a paying adult.

DISABLED INFORMATION
Wheelchairs: 15 spaces available, accommodated below the Grandstand
Helpers: One helper admitted per disabled fan
Prices: Normal prices for the disabled. Free for helpers
Disabled Toilets: One available
Contact: (01475) 723571 (Bookings are necessary) – Andy Adams (Disability Officer) – admin@gmfc.net

Travelling Supporters' Information:
Routes: From the North: Take the M8 to the A8. From Port Glasgow follow the A78 to Greenock. Cappielow Park is on the left after passing under the railway bridge; From the South: Take the A78 to Greenock. Follow the road past IBM then turn right at the second set of lights into Dunlop Street. Follow this road until it turns sharp left and goes downhill and continue to the traffic lights facing the river. Turn right onto the A8, cross two roundabouts and Cappielow Park is on the right hand side of the road.

HAMILTON ACADEMICAL FC

Founded: 1874 (**Entered League**: 1897)
Nickname: 'The Accies'
Ground: The ZLX Stadium, New Douglas Park, Cadzow Avenue, Hamilton   ML3 0FT
Ground Capacity: 6,017 (all seats)
Record Attendance: 6,007 (17th January 2015)

Colours: Red and White hooped shirts, White shorts
Telephone Nº: (01698) 368650
Website: www.hamiltonacciesfc.co.uk
E-mail: office@acciesfc.co.uk

GENERAL INFORMATION
Car Parking: In Caird Street Council Car Park (400 yards)
Coach Parking: In Caird Street Car Park (400 yards)
Nearest Railway Station: Hamilton West (200 yards)
Nearest Bus Station: Hamilton (1 mile)
Club Shop: At the stadium
Opening Times: Weekdays 9.30am to 5.00pm
Telephone Nº: (01698) 368650 or 368658

GROUND INFORMATION
Away Supporters' Entrances & Sections:
North and East Stands – use turnstiles 7 to 12

ADMISSION INFO (2024/2025+ PRICES)
Adult Seating: £26.00
Under-18s Seating: £16.00
Under-16s Seating: £8.00
Senior Citizen Seating: £16.00

DISABLED INFORMATION
Wheelchairs: Accommodated in the front row of the stand or by the trackside
Helpers: Admitted following prior booking
Prices: Normal prices for the disabled. Helpers admitted free.
Disabled Toilets: Available in the Main Stand and beside turnstiles 4 to 6 for Away supporters
Contact: (01698) 368650 (Bookings are necessary)

Travelling Supporters' Information:
Routes: Exit the M74 at Junction 5 and follow signs marked "Football Traffic". Go past Hamilton Racecourse, turn right at the lights by Hamilton Business Park then first right again for New Park Street and Auchinraith Avenue. The ground is behind Morrisons and Sainsburys.

LIVINGSTON FC

Founded: 1943 (**Entered League**: 1974)
Former Names: Ferranti Thistle FC, Meadowbank Thistle FC
Nickname: 'The Lions'
Ground: Tony Macaroni Arena, Alderstone Road, Livingston EH54 7DN
Ground Capacity: 9,512 (All seats)

Record Attendance: 10,112 (vs Rangers, 27/10/01)
Colours: Amber shirts, shorts and socks
Telephone Nº: (01506) 417000
Website: www.livingstonfc.co.uk
E-mail: secretary@livingstonfc.co.uk

GENERAL INFORMATION
Car Parking: At the ground on a first-come, first-served basis. Otherwise, fans should park in the Town Centre.
Coach Parking: At the ground
Nearest Railway Station: Livingston
Nearest Bus Station: Livingston
Club Shop: At the Stadium
Opening Times: Daily – please phone for further details
Telephone Nº: (01506) 238010
E-mail: livingstonfc@clubstore.co.uk

GROUND INFORMATION
Away Supporters' Entrances & Sections:
East Stand entrances and accommodation

ADMISSION INFO (2024/2025 PRICES)
Adult Seating: £24.00
Concessionary Seating: £16.00
Ages 16 to 18 Seating: £13.00
Under-16s Seating: £9.00

DISABLED INFORMATION
Wheelchairs: Accommodated
Helpers: Admitted
Prices: Normal prices for fans with disabilities. Helpers are admitted free of charge.
Disabled Toilets: Available
Contact: (01506) 417000 (Bookings are necessary)
E-mail: dao@livingstonfc.co.uk

Travelling Supporters' Information:
Routes: Exit the M8 at the Livingston turn-off and take the A899 to the Cousland Interchange. Turn right into Cousland Road, pass the Hospital, then turn left into Alderstone Road and the stadium is on the left opposite the Campus.

PARTICK THISTLE FC

Founded: 1876 (**Entered League**: 1890)
Nickname: 'The Jags'
Ground: Wyre Stadium@Firhill, 80 Firhill Road, Glasgow G20 7AL
Ground Capacity: 10,102 (All seats)
Record Attendance: 49,838 (18th February 1922)

Colours: Red and Yellow shirts with Black shorts
Telephone Nº: (0141) 579-1971
Ticket Office: (0141) 579-1971 Option 1
Website: www.ptfc.co.uk
E-mail: mail@ptfc.co.uk

GENERAL INFORMATION
Car Parking: Street parking
Coach Parking: Panmure Street
Nearest Railway Station: Possilpark & Parkhouse (1¼ miles)
Nearest Underground Station: St. George's Cross
Club Shops: At the ground
Opening Times: Matchdays only, 1 hour before kick-off
Telephone Nº: (0141) 579-1971 (Option 2)

GROUND INFORMATION
Away Supporters' Entrances & Sections:
North End of the Jackie Husband Stand and also in the Colin Weir Stand, depending on the size of the travelling support.

ADMISSION INFO (2024/2025 PRICES)
Adult Seating: £20.00
Concessionary Seating: £15.00
Under-16s Seating: £5.00

DISABLED INFORMATION
Wheelchairs: 17 spaces in the John Lambie Stand
Helpers: One helper admitted per wheelchair
Prices: £15.00 for each disabled fan plus one helper
Disabled Toilets: Available in the John Lambie Stand, Colin Weir Stand and Jackie Husband Stand
Contact: (0141) 579-1971 or dao@ptfc.co.uk (Dougie McInnes) (Bookings are necessary)

Travelling Supporters' Information:
Routes: From the East: Exit the M8 at Junction 16; From the West: Exit the M8 at Junction 17. From both directions, follow Maryhill Road to Queen's Cross and the ground is on the right.

QUEEN'S PARK FC   (HAMPDEN PARK)

Founded: 1867   (**Entered League**: 1900)
Nickname: 'The Spiders'
Ground: The City Stadium, Mount Florida, Glasgow, G42 9BA
Ground Capacity: 951   (All seats)

Colours: Black and White hooped shirts, White shorts
Telephone/Ticket Office N°: (0141) 632-1275
Website: www.queensparkfc.co.uk
E-mail: generalenquiries@queensparkfc.co.uk

GENERAL INFORMATION
Car Parking: Car park at the Stadium
Coach Parking: Car park at the Stadium
Nearest Railway Station: Mount Florida and King's Park (both 5 minutes walk)
Nearest Bus Station: Buchanan Street
Club Shop: At the ground
Opening Times: During home matches only
Telephone N°: (0141) 632-1275

GROUND INFORMATION
Away Supporters' Entrances & Sections:
South Stand – Section P

ADMISSION INFO (2024/2025 PRICES)
Adult Seating: £22.00
Concessionary Seating: £15.00
Under-18s Seating: £10.00
Under-12s Seating: £6.00

DISABLED INFORMATION
Wheelchairs: Accommodated
Helpers: Admitted
Prices: Free for both the disabled and helpers
Disabled Toilets: Available
Contact: (0141) 632-1275   (Mhairi Gordon)

Travelling Supporters' Information:
Routes: From the South: Take the A724 to the Cambuslang Road and at Eastfield branch left into Main Street and follow through Burnhill Street and Westmuir Place into Prospecthill Road. Turn left into Aikenhead Road and right into Mount Annan for Kinghorn Drive and the Stadium; From the South: Take the A77 Fenwick Road, through Kilmarnock Road into Pollokshaws Road then turn right into Langside Avenue. Pass through Battle Place to Battlefield Road and turn left into Cathcart Road. Turn right into Letherby Drive, right into Carmunnock Road and 1st left into Mount Annan Drive for the Stadium; From the North & East: Exit M8 Junction 15 and passing Infirmary on left proceed into High Street and cross the Albert Bridge into Crown Street. Join Cathcart Road and proceed South until it becomes Carmunnock Road. Turn left into Mount Annan Drive and left again into Kinghorn Drive for the Stadium.

RAITH ROVERS FC

Founded: 1883 (**Entered League**: 1902)
Nickname: 'The Rovers'
Ground: Stark's Park, Pratt Street, Kirkcaldy, KY1 1SA
Ground Capacity: 8,867 (All seats)
Record Attendance: 31,306 (7th February 1953)

Colours: Navy Blue shirts with White shorts
Telephone N°: (01592) 263514
Ticket Office: (01592) 263514
Website: www.raithrovers.net
E-mail: info@raithrovers.net

GENERAL INFORMATION
Car Parking: Esplanade and Beveridge Car Park
Coach Parking: Railway Station & Esplanade
Nearest Railway Station: Kirkcaldy (15 minutes walk)
Nearest Bus Station: Kirkcaldy (15 minutes walk)
Club Shop: At the ground (South Stand)
Opening Times: Monday to Friday and Saturday Matchdays 9.00am to 4.00pm
Telephone N°: (01592) 263514 (Option 2)

GROUND INFORMATION
Away Supporters' Entrances & Sections:
McDermid (North) Stand

ADMISSION INFO (2024/2025 PRICES)
Adult Seating: £22.00 – £24.00
Concessionary Seating: £14.00 – £16.00
Under-21s Seating: £13.00 – £15.00
Under-16s Seating: £8.00 – £10.00
Under-12s Seating: Free with a paying adult

DISABLED INFORMATION
Wheelchairs: 14 spaces each for home and away fans accommodated in the McDermid and Penman Family Stand
Helpers: One helper admitted per wheelchair
Prices: Disabled fans receive a 50% discount on usual matchday prices. Helpers are admitted free of charge
Disabled Toilets: Available in the North and South Stands
Contact: (01592) 263514 Evelyn Hood (Disability Officer) (Bookings are necessary for all-ticket games)
E-mail: slo@raithrovers.net

Travelling Supporters' Information:
Routes: Take the M8 to the end then follow the A90/M90 over the Forth Road Bridge. Exit the M90 at Junction 1 and follow the A921 to Kirkcaldy. On the outskirts of town, turn left at the B & Q roundabout from which the floodlights can be seen. The ground is raised on the hill nearby.

THE SCOTTISH PROFESSIONAL FOOTBALL LEAGUE

WILLIAM HILL SCOTTISH LEAGUE ONE

Address
National Stadium, Hampden Park,
Mount Florida, Glasgow   G42 9DE

Website   www.spfl.co.uk
E-mail   info@spfl.co.uk
Phone   (0141) 620-4140

Clubs for the 2024-2025 Season

Alloa Athletic FC .... Page 28
Annan Athletic FC .... Page 29
Arbroath FC .... Page 30
Cove Rangers FC .... Page 31
Dumbarton FC .... Page 32
Inverness Caledonian Thistle FC .... Page 33
Kelty Hearts FC .... Page 34
Montrose FC .... Page 35
Queen of the South FC .... Page 36
Stenhousemuir FC .... Page 37

ALLOA ATHLETIC FC

Founded: 1878 (**Entered League**: 1921)
Nickname: 'The Wasps'
Ground: The Indodrill Stadium, Clackmannan Road, Alloa FK10 1RY
Ground Capacity: 3,100
Seating Capacity: 905
Record Attendance: 15,467 (vs Celtic, February 1939)

Colours: Gold and Black shirts with Black shorts
Telephone Nº: (01259) 722695
Ticket Office: (01259) 722695
Website: www.alloaathletic.co.uk
E-mail: fcadmin@alloaathletic.co.uk

GENERAL INFORMATION
Car Parking: Street parking only
Coach Parking: By Police Direction
Nearest Railway Station: Alloa
Nearest Bus Station: Alloa
Club Shop: At the ground
Opening Times: Matchdays only 1.30pm to 5.00pm
Telephone Nº: (01259) 722695

GROUND INFORMATION
Away Supporters' Entrances & Sections:
Hilton Road entrance for the Hilton Road Side

ADMISSION INFO (2024/2025 PRICES)
Adult Standing/Standing: £20.00
Senior Citizen Standing/Seating: £12.00
Under-16s Standing/Seating: £6.00

DISABLED INFORMATION
Wheelchairs: Accommodated in the Disabled Section underneath the Main Stand
Helpers: Admitted
Prices: Concessionary prices for the disabled. Free for helpers
Disabled Toilets: One available in both the Main Stand and the away supporters' section
Contact: (01259) 722695 (Bookings are not necessary) – Robert Wilson (Disability Officer): fcadmin@alloaathletic.co.uk

Travelling Supporters' Information:
Routes: From the South and East: Take the M74 to the M80 and exit at Junction 9 following the A907 into Alloa. Continue over two roundabouts passing the brewery and Town Centre. The Ground is on the left-hand side of the road.

ANNAN ATHLETIC FC

Founded: 1942
Former Names: Solway Star FC
Nickname: 'Galabankies'
Ground: Galabank, North Street, Annan, Dumfries & Galloway DG12 5DG
Record Attendance: 2,517 (vs Rangers)

Ground Capacity: 2,504
Seating Capacity: 500
Colours: Gold shirts with Black shorts and Gold socks
Telephone Nº: (01461) 204108
Website: www.annanathleticfc.com
E-mail: exec@annanathleticfc.com

GENERAL INFORMATION
Car Parking: Available at the ground
Coach Parking: Available at the ground
Nearest Railway Station: Annan
Nearest Bus Station: Annan
Club Shop: At the ground
Opening Times: Saturdays between 3.00pm and 6.00pm
Telephone Nº: (01461) 204108

GROUND INFORMATION
Away Supporters' Entrances & Sections:
North Stand

ADMISSION INFO (2024/2025 PRICES)
Adult Standing/Seating: £16.00
Concessionary Standing/Seating: £12.00
Ages 12 to 16 Standing/Seating: £6.00
Under-12s Standing/Seating: free with paying Adult

DISABLED INFORMATION
Wheelchairs: Accommodated
Helpers: Admitted
Prices: Concessionary prices are charged for disabled fans. Helpers are admitted free of charge
Disabled Toilets: Available
Contact: (01461) 204108   (Bookings are necessary) secretary@annanathleticfc.com

Travelling Supporters' Information:
Routes: From the East: Take the A75 to Annan. Approaching Annan, exit onto the B6357 (Stapleton Road) and after ¾ mile take the second exit at the roundabout into Scotts Street. Continue into Church Street and High Street. Turn right into Lady Street (B722) and following along into North Street for the ground; From the West: Take the A75 to Annan and turn right onto the B721 through Howes and into High Street in Annan (1 mile). After about 300 yards turn left into Lady Street. Then as above.

ARBROATH FC

Founded: 1878 (**Entered League**: 1902)
Nickname: 'The Red Lichties'
Ground: The Greenversity Stadium
@Gayfield, Arbroath DD11 1QJ
Ground Capacity: 6,600   **Seating Capacity**: 861
Record Attendance: 13,510 (23rd February 1952)

Colours: Maroon shirts and white shorts
Telephone Nº: (01241) 872157
Ticket Office: (01241) 872157
Website: www.arbroathfc.co.uk
E-mail: office@arbroathfc.co.uk

GENERAL INFORMATION
Car Parking: Car Park in Queen's Drive
Coach Parking: Car Park in Queen's Drive
Nearest Railway Station: Arbroath (15 minutes walk)
Nearest Bus Station: Arbroath (10 minutes walk)
Club Shop: At the ground
Opening Times: Matchdays only 2.00pm – 5.00pm
Telephone Nº: (01241) 872157

GROUND INFORMATION
Away Supporters' Entrances & Sections:
Queen's Drive End

ADMISSION INFO (2024/2025 PRICES)
Adult Standing: £18.00
Adult Seating: £19.00
Concessionary Standing: £13.00
Concessionary Seating: £14.00
Family Standing Ticket: £21.00 – £23.00
Family Seating Ticket: £22.00 – £25.00

DISABLED INFORMATION
Wheelchairs: 6 spaces available at both of the West and East Ends of the Main Stand
Helpers: Admitted
Prices: Free for the disabled. Normal prices for helpers
Disabled Toilets: Two available at the rear of the Stand
Contact: (01241) 872157 (Bookings are not necessary)

Travelling Supporters' Information:
Routes: From Dundee and the West: Take the A92 (Coast Road). On entering Arbroath, pass under the Railway Line and the ground is on the right-hand side; From Stonehaven/Montrose: Take the A92, pass through Arbroath, go past the Harbour and the ground is on the left-hand side.

COVE RANGERS FC

Founded: 1922 (**Entered League**: 2019)
Nickname: None
Former Ground: Balmoral Stadium, Wellington Circle, Altens, Aberdeen AB12 3JG
Ground Capacity: 3,023
Seating Capacity: 2,012

Record Attendance: 1,955 (11th May 2019)
Colours: Blue shirts and shorts
Telephone Nº: (01224) 392111
Website: www.coverangersfc.com
E-mail: info@coverangersfc.com

GENERAL INFORMATION
Car Parking: At the ground & street parking
Coach Parking: At the ground
Nearest Railway Station: Aberdeen (3 miles)
Nearest Bus Station: Aberdeen (3 miles)
Club Shop: In the 'Fan's Bar' at the stadium
Opening Times: Matchdays only
Telephone Nº: (01224) 392111

GROUND INFORMATION
Away Supporters' Entrances & Sections:
No usual segregation

ADMISSION INFO (2024/2025 PRICES)
Adult Standing: £15.00
Adult Seating: £17.00
Concessionary Standing: £9.00
Concessionary Seating: £10.00
Ages 12 to 16 Standing: £6.00
Ages 12 to 16 Seating: £7.00
Note: Under-12s are admitted free with a paying adult

DISABLED INFORMATION
Wheelchairs: 2 spaces available in total
Helpers: Admitted
Prices: Normal prices apply for disabled fans
Disabled Toilets: Available
Contact: (01224) 392111   Please contact the club for further information and to arrange bookings.

Travelling Supporters' Information:
Routes: The stadium is situated in Calder Park in the Altens district of Aberdeen. Travelling from the north or south, take the A90 to the southern part of Aberdeen then exit onto the A956 Wellington Road and follow north towards Altens. After 1¼ miles, turn left at the roundabout by the Burger King into Wellington Circle and follow the road round past Ikea, Makro and the Royal Mail depot for the ground.

DUMBARTON FC

Founded: 1872 (**Entered League**: 1890)
Nickname: 'Sons'
Ground: C & G Systems Stadium, Castle Road, Dumbarton G82 1JJ
Ground Capacity: 2,025 (All seats)
Record Attendance: 1,978 (vs Rangers 2015)

Colours: Yellow and Black striped shirts, Black shorts
Telephone N°: (01389) 762569
Ticket Office: (01389) 762569
Website: www.dumbartonfootballclub.com
E-mail: office@dumbartonfc.co.uk

GENERAL INFORMATION
Car Parking: 500 spaces available at the ground (£3.00)
Coach Parking: At the ground
Nearest Railway Station: Dumbarton East
Nearest Bus Station: Dumbarton
Club Shop: At the ground
Opening Times: Monday, Wednesday and Friday 9.30am to 1.30pm plus Saturday matchdays 11.00am to 5.00pm
Telephone N°: (01389) 762569

GROUND INFORMATION
Away Supporters' Entrances & Sections:
West Sections 1 and 2

ADMISSION INFO (2024/2025 PRICES)
Adult Seating: £17.00
Concessionary Seating: £11.00
Under-16s Seating: £5.00

DISABLED INFORMATION
Wheelchairs: Approximately 24 spaces available in the disabled area
Prices: Concessionary prices apply for disabled fans. Helpers are admitted free of charge
Disabled Toilets: Available
Contact: (01389) 762569 (Bookings are necessary)

Travelling Supporters' Information:
Routes: The ground is situated just by Dumbarton Castle. Take the A814 into Dumbarton and follow the brown signs for the Castle to find the ground.

INVERNESS CALEDONIAN THISTLE FC

Founded: 1994 (**Entered League**: 1994)
Former Names: Caledonian Thistle FC
Nickname: 'The Jags' 'Caley'
Ground: Tulloch Caledonian Stadium, Stadium Road, Inverness   IV1 1FF
Ground Capacity: 7,512 (all seats)
Record Attendance: 7,753 (vs Rangers, 2005)

Colours: Shirts are Royal Blue and Red, Shorts are Royal Blue
Telephone Nº: (01463) 222880 (Ground)
Ticket Office: (01463) 227451
Website: www.ictfc.co.uk
E-mail: admin@ictfc.co.uk

GENERAL INFORMATION
Car Parking: Chargeable parking available at the ground
Coach Parking: At the ground
Nearest Railway Station: Inverness (1 mile)
Nearest Bus Station: Inverness
Club Shop: At the ground
Opening Times: Weekdays 9.00am to 5.00pm and Matchdays 9.00am until kick-off
Telephone Nº: (01463) 227451

GROUND INFORMATION
Away Supporters' Entrances & Sections:
South Stand

ADMISSION INFO (2024/2025 PRICES)
Adult Seating: £22.00 – £24.00
Under-16s Seating: £8.00
Senior Citizen/Ages 16 to 22 Seating: £17.00 – £19.00

DISABLED INFORMATION
Wheelchairs: 52 spaces available in total
Helpers: Admitted
Prices: Normal prices for disabled fans. Helpers admitted free
Disabled Toilets: Available
Contact: (01463) 222880   (Bookings are necessary)
David Scott (Access Officer): dao@ictfc.co.uk

Travelling Supporters' Information:
Routes: The ground is adjacent to Kessock Bridge. From the South: Take the A9 to Inverness and turn right at the roundabout before the bridge over the Moray Firth; From the North: Take the A9 over the bridge and turn left at the roundabout for the ground.

KELTY HEARTS FC

Founded: 1975
Nickname: 'The Hearts' and 'The Jambo's'
Ground: New Central Park, Bath Street, Kelty, KY4 0AG
Ground Capacity: 2,181
Seating Capacity: 353
Record Attendance: 2,300 (vs Rangers XI)

Colours: Maroon shirts with White shorts
Telephone Nº: (01383) 830844 (Social Club)
Contact Nº: 07982 725903
Website: www.keltyhearts.co.uk
E-mail: enquiries@keltyhearts.co.uk

GENERAL INFORMATION
Car Parking: At the ground
Coach Parking: At the ground
Nearest Railway Station: Cowdenbeath (2¾ miles)
Nearest Bus Station: Cowdenbeath
Club Shop: At the ground
Opening Times: Matchdays only
Telephone Nº: (01383) 830844 (Social Club)

GROUND INFORMATION
Away Supporters' Entrances & Sections:
No usual segregation

ADMISSION INFO (2024/2025 PRICES)
Adult Standing/Seating: £16.00 – £18.00
Concessionary Standing/Seating: £12.00 – £13.00
Under-16s Standing/Seating: £5.00 – £6.00

DISABLED INFORMATION
Wheelchairs: Accommodated
Helpers: Admitted
Prices: Free of charge for disabled fans. Half-price for helpers
Disabled Toilets: 2 available
Contact: 07982 725903 (Bookings are not necessary)

Travelling Supporters' Information:
Routes: Exit the M90 at Junction 4 and take the A909 Cocklaw Street into Kelty. Turn left at the roundabout onto Main Street then 2nd right into Bath Street. Turn left just past the houses for the road to New Central Park.

MONTROSE FC

Founded: 1879 (**Entered League**: 1929)
Nickname: 'Gable Endies'
Ground: Links Park Stadium, Wellington Street, Montrose   DD10 8QD
Ground Capacity: 4,936
Seating Capacity: 1,338
Record Attendance: 8,983 (vs Dundee – 17/3/1973)

Colours: Blue shirts with White Sleeves, Blue shorts
Telephone Nº: (01674) 673200
Ticket Office: (01674) 673200
Website: www.montrosefc.co.uk
E-mail: office@montrosefc.co.uk

GENERAL INFORMATION
Car Parking: At the ground and Street parking also
Coach Parking: Mid-Links (5 minutes walk)
Nearest Railway Station: Montrose Western Road
Nearest Bus Station: High Street, Montrose
Club Shop: At the ground
Opening Times: Matchdays 10.00am to 3.00pm and also on Monday and Wednesday evenings
Telephone Nº: (01674) 673200 or 07923 673775

GROUND INFORMATION
Away Supporters' Entrances & Sections:
No usual segregation

ADMISSION INFO (2024/2025 PRICES)
Adults Standing/Seating: £18.00
Concessions Standing/Seating: £10.00
Under-12s Standing/Seating: Free with paying adult

DISABLED INFORMATION
Wheelchairs: 5 spaces available in the Main Stand
Helpers: Admitted
Prices: Concessionary prices are charged for disabled fans. Helpers are admitted free of charge
Disabled Toilets: 2 available in the Main Stand
Contact: (01674) 673200 (Bookings are helpful) – Kevin Watson or Stephen McCallum (Liaison Officers)

Travelling Supporters' Information:
Routes: Take the main A92 Coastal Road to Montrose. Once in the town, the ground is well signposted and is situated in the Mid-Links area.

QUEEN OF THE SOUTH FC

Founded: 1919 (**Entered League**: 1923)
Nickname: 'The Doonhamers'
Ground: Palmerston Park, Terregles Street, Dumfries DG2 9BA
Ground Capacity: 8,690
Seating Capacity: 3,377
Record Attendance: 26,552 (23rd February 1952)

Colours: Blue shirts with White shorts
Telephone Nº: (01387) 254853
Ticket Office: (01387) 254853
Website: www.qosfc.com
E-mail: admin@qosfc.com

GENERAL INFORMATION
Car Parking: Car Park adjacent to the ground
Coach Parking: Car Park adjacent to the ground
Nearest Railway Station: Dumfries (¾ mile)
Nearest Bus Station: Dumfries Whitesands (5 minutes walk)
Club Shop: At the ground
Opening Times: Weekdays 9.00am to 4.00pm and Saturday Matchdays 11.30am – 3.00pm + 4.45pm – 5.05pm
Telephone Nº: (01387) 254853

GROUND INFORMATION
Away Supporters' Entrances & Sections:
BDS Digital Stand/Terregles Street entrances for the East Stand

ADMISSION INFO (2024/2025 PRICES)
Adult Standing/Seating: £18.00
Senior Citizen/Ages 16 to 21 Standing/Seating: £10.00
Under-16s Standing/Seating: £5.00

DISABLED INFORMATION
Wheelchairs: Accommodated in front of the East Stand
Prices: Free of charge for helpers. Prices for the disabled are £8.00 for Adults, Concessions £5.00 and Under-16s £3.00.
Disabled Toilets: Available
Contact: (01387) 254853 (Bookings are not necessary except for games against Rangers FC) – Keith Thom (Disability Officer): dao@qosfc.com

Travelling Supporters' Information:
Routes: From the East: Take the A75 to Dumfries and follow the ring road over the River Nith. Turn left at the 1st roundabout then right at the 2nd roundabout (the Kilmarnock/Glasgow Road roundabout). The ground is a short way along past the Tesco store; From the West: Take the A75 to Dumfries and proceed along ring road to the 1st roundabout (Kilmarnock/Glasgow Road) then as from the East; From the North: Take A76 to Dumfries and carry straight across 1st roundabout for the ground.

STENHOUSEMUIR FC

Founded: 1884 (**Entered League**: 1921)
Former Names: Heather Rangers FC
Nickname: 'Warriors'
Ground: Ochilview Park, Gladstone Road, Stenhousemuir FK5 4QL
Ground Capacity: 3,746
Seating Capacity: 626

Record Attendance: 12,500 (11th March 1950)
Colours: Maroon shirts with White shorts
Telephone Nº: (01324) 562992
Website: www.stenhousemuirfc.com
E-mail: info@stenhousemuirfc.com

GENERAL INFORMATION
Car Parking: Street parking only
Coach Parking: Tryst Showground (adjacent)
Nearest Railway Station: Larbert (1 mile)
Nearest Bus Station: Falkirk (2½ miles)
Club Shop: At the ground
Opening Times: Weekdays from 9.00am to 5.00pm (closed Wednesday afternoons) and also from 2.00pm on Saturday matchdays
Telephone Nº: (01324) 562992

GROUND INFORMATION
Away Supporters' Entrances & Sections: Terracing entrances and accommodation

ADMISSION INFO (2024/2025 PRICES)
Adult Standing: £18.00
Adult Seating: £18.00
Senior Citizen/Concessionary Standing: £13.00
Senior Citizen/Concessionary Seating: £13.00
Under-16s Standing/Seating: £5.00

DISABLED INFORMATION
Wheelchairs: Accommodated
Helpers: Admitted
Prices: Free for disabled fans. Concessionary prices are charged for helpers
Disabled Toilets: Available in the Gladstone Road Stand
Contact: (01324) 562992 (Bookings are not necessary)

Travelling Supporters' Information:
Routes: Exit the M876 at Junction 2 and follow signs for Stenhousemuir. Pass the Old Hospital and turn right after the Golf Course. The ground is on the left behind the houses – the floodlights are visible for ¼ mile.

THE SCOTTISH PROFESSIONAL FOOTBALL LEAGUE

WILLIAM HILL SCOTTISH LEAGUE TWO

Address
National Stadium, Hampden Park,
Mount Florida, Glasgow   G42 9DE

Website www.spfl.co.uk
E-mail info@spfl.co.uk
Phone (0141) 620-4140

Clubs for the 2024-2025 Season

Bonnyrigg Rose FC .... Page 39
Clyde FC .... Page 40
East Fife FC .... Page 41
Edinburgh City FC .... Page 42
Elgin City FC .... Page 43
Forfar Athletic FC .... Page 44
Peterhead FC .... Page 45
Stirling Albion FC .... Page 46
Stranraer FC .... Page 47
The Spartans FC .... Page 48

BONNYRIGG ROSE ATHLETIC FC

Photograph courtesy of Waluna Productions

Founded: 1881
Nickname: 'The Rose'
Ground: New Dundas Park, Bonnyrigg, Midlothian, EH19 3AE
Ground Capacity: 2,200 **Seating Capacity**: None
Record Attendance: 3,000

Colours: Red and White hooped shirts, White shorts
Telephone N°: (0131) 663-7702
Contact E-mail: contact@bonnyriggrose.org.uk
Website: www.bonnyriggrose.org.uk
E-mail: contact@bonnyriggrose.org.uk

GENERAL INFORMATION
Car Parking: At the ground plus street parking
Coach Parking: Please contact the club for details
Nearest Railway Station: Eskbank (1 mile)
Nearest Bus Station: Bonnyrigg Toll
Social Club: At New Dundas Park
Opening Times: Thursdays 7.00pm until midnight, Friday and Saturday 11.00am to 1.00am and Sunday 11.00am until midnight.
Telephone N°: (0131) 663-7036

GROUND INFORMATION
Away Supporters' Entrances & Sections:
No usual segregation

ADMISSION INFO (2024/2025 PRICES)
Adults: £15.00
Concessions: £10.00
Ages 12 to 16: £5.00
Under-12s: Free of charge with a paying adult

DISABLED INFORMATION
Wheelchairs: Accommodated
Helpers: Admitted
Prices: Concessionary prices are charged for disabled fans, helpers are admitted free of charge
Disabled Toilets: 2 available close to the Lothian Street entrance
Contact: (0131) 663-7702 (Bookings are appreciated)

Travelling Supporters' Information:
Routes: Access to the ground is via the social club which is situated just off Dundas Street (B704), near the junction with Lothian Street (A6094). From the North or South: Take the A7 then exit at the Eskbank Road Roundabout onto the A6094 Eskbank Road, heading into Bonnyrigg. Continue for approximately 1 mile (the road continues into Lothian Street), then turn left at the traffic lights onto the B704 Dundas Steet and immediately left again at the Calderwood Inn for the Social Club.

CLYDE FC

Clyde FC are groundsharing with Hamilton Academical FC during the 2024/2025 season.

Founded: 1877 (**Entered League**: 1906)
Nickname: 'Bully Wee'
Ground: The ZLX Stadium, New Douglas Park, Cadzow Avenue, Hamilton ML3 0FT
Ground Capacity: 6,017 (all seats)

Colours: White Shirts with Black shorts
Telephone N°: (01236) 451511 (Matchdays only)
Ticket Office: (01236) 451511
Website: www.clydefc.co.uk
E-mail: info@clydefc.co.uk

GENERAL INFORMATION
Car Parking: In Caird Street Council Car Park (400 yards)
Coach Parking: In Caird Street Car Park (400 yards)
Nearest Railway Station: Hamilton West (200 yards)
Nearest Bus Station: Hamilton (1 mile)
Club Shop: Order via club website

GROUND INFORMATION
Away Supporters' Entrances & Sections:
North and East Stands – use turnstiles 7 to 12

ADMISSION INFO (2024/2025 PRICES)
Adult Seating: £19.00
Under-18s Seating: £5.00
Senior Citizen Seating: £15.00

DISABLED INFORMATION
Wheelchairs: Accommodated in the front row of the stand or by the trackside
Helpers: Admitted following prior booking
Prices: Normal prices for the disabled. Helpers admitted free.
Disabled Toilets: Available in the Main Stand and beside turnstiles 4 to 6 for Away supporters
Contact: dao@clydefc.co.uk

Travelling Supporters' Information:
Routes: Exit the M74 at Junction 5 and follow signs marked "Football Traffic". Go past Hamilton Racecourse, turn right at the lights by Hamilton Business Park then first right again for New Park Street and Auchinraith Avenue. The ground is behind Morrisons and Sainsburys.

EAST FIFE FC

Founded: 1903 (**Entered League**: 1903)
Nickname: 'The Fife'
Ground: MGM Timber Bayview Stadium, Harbour View, Methil, Fife KY8 3RW
Ground Capacity: 1,980 (All seats)
Record Attendance: 22,515 (2nd January 1950)

Colours: Gold and Black shirts with White shorts
Telephone Nº: (01333) 426323
Ticket Office: (01333) 426323
Website: www.eastfifefc.info
E-mail: office@eastfifefc.info

GENERAL INFORMATION
Car Parking: Adjacent to the ground
Coach Parking: Adjacent to the ground
Nearest Railway Station: Kirkcaldy (8 miles)
Nearest Bus Station: Leven
Club Shop: At the ground
Opening Times: Monday to Thursday 9.15am to 4.45pm, Friday 9.15am to 3.45pm and also on Saturday matchdays
Telephone Nº: (01333) 426323

GROUND INFORMATION
Away Supporters' Entrances & Sections: Accommodated within the Main Stand

ADMISSION INFO (2024/2025 PRICES)
Adult Seating: £18.00
Under-16s Seating: £5.00
Concessionary Seating: £14.00
Note: Family tickets are also available

DISABLED INFORMATION
Wheelchairs: 24 spaces available in total
Helpers: Admitted
Prices: Concessionary prices for the disabled. Helpers free
Disabled Toilets: Yes
Contact: (01333) 426323 (Bookings are necessary) – Stephen Mill (Disability Officer) 07845 451554 office@eastfifefc.info

Travelling Supporters' Information:
Routes: Take the A915 from Kirkcaldy past Buckhaven and Methil to Leven. Turn right at the traffic lights and go straight on at the first roundabout then turn right at the second roundabout. Cross Bawbee Bridge and turn left at the next roundabout. The ground is the first turning on the left after ¼ mile.

EDINBURGH CITY FC

Founded: 1928 (re-formed 1986)
Nickname: 'The Citizens'
Ground: Meadowbank Stadium, London Road, Edinburgh, EH7 6AE
Ground Capacity: 1,280
Seating Capacity: 499

Record Attendance: 5,740 (1936, at City Park)
Colours: White shirts and shorts
Telephone N°: (0131) 210-0478
Website: www.edinburghcityfc.com
E-mail: hello@edinburghcityfc.com

GENERAL INFORMATION
Social Club: 74 Lochend Road South, Edinburgh EH7 6DR
Telephone N°: 0845 463-1932
Nearest Railway Station: Edinburgh Waverley (1.4 miles)
Buses: Services 4, 5 & 26 all stock at the Sports Centre bus stop which is on London Road close by.
Club Shop: Please order via the club website

GROUND INFORMATION
Away Supporters' Entrances & Sections:
No segregation

ADMISSION INFO (2024/2025 PRICES)
Adult Standing/Seating: £15.00
Concessionary Standing/Seating: £10.00
Note: Under-12s are admitted for £5.00 with a paying adult

DISABLED INFORMATION
Wheelchairs: Accommodated
Helpers: Admitted
Prices: Concessionary prices apply for fans with disabilities. Helpers are admitted free of charge
Disabled Toilets: Available
Contact: andy@edinburghcityfc.com

Travelling Supporters' Information:
Routes: Meadowbank Sports Centre is located directly on the A1 (London Road) close to the Palace of Holyroodhouse which is signposted throughout the city.

ELGIN CITY FC

Founded: 1893 (**Entered League**: 2000)
Nickname: 'Black and Whites'
Ground: Borough Briggs, Borough Briggs Road, Elgin IV30 1AP
Ground Capacity: 4,520
Seating Capacity: 478
Record Attendance: 12,608 (17th February 1968)

Colours: Black and White Striped shirts, Black shorts
Telephone Nº: (01343) 551114
Ticket Information: (01343) 551114
Website: www.elgincity.net
E-mail: vicky.duguid@elgincityfc.co.uk

GENERAL INFORMATION
Car Parking: Lossie Green Car Park (2 minutes walk)
Coach Parking: Lossie Green Car Park (2 minutes walk)
Nearest Railway Station: Elgin (1 mile)
Nearest Bus Station: Elgin (¼ mile)
Club Shop: At the ground
Opening Times: Weekdays 9.30am to 4.30pm and also Saturdays 12.30am to 5.00pm (home matchdays only)
Telephone Nº: (01343) 551114

GROUND INFORMATION
Away Supporters' Entrances & Sections:
West End entrances for the Covered Enclosure

ADMISSION INFO (2024/2025 PRICES)
Adult Standing: £16.00
Adult Seating: £18.00
Concessionary Standing: £10.00
Concessionary Seating: £12.00
Under-16s Standing/Seating: Free of charge with a paying Adult.

DISABLED INFORMATION
Wheelchairs: Accommodated in both home and away ends
Helpers: Admitted
Prices: Concessionary prices charged for disabled fans
Disabled Toilets: Available in the East Side of the stadium
Contact: (01343) 551114   (Bookings are not necessary)

Travelling Supporters' Information:
Routes: Take the Alexandra bypass to the roundabout ½ mile from the City Centre and turn left towards Lossiemouth. Borough Briggs Road is on the left.

FORFAR ATHLETIC FC

Founded: 1885 (**Entered League**: 1921)
Nickname: 'Loons'
Ground: The Alpha Projects Stadium@Station Park, Carseview Road, Forfar, Angus   DD8 3BT
Ground Capacity: 6,777
Seating Capacity: 739
Record Attendance: 10,780 (2nd February 1970)

Colours: Sky Blue shirts with White shorts
Telephone Nº: (01307) 463576
Ticket Office: (01307) 463576
Website: www.forfarathletic.co.uk
E-mail: alan.shepherd@forfarathletic.co.uk

GENERAL INFORMATION
Car Parking: Market Muir Car Park and adjacent streets
Coach Parking: Market Muir Car Park
Nearest Railway Station: Dundee or Arbroath (14 miles)
Nearest Bus Station: Forfar (½ mile)
Club Shop: At the ground
Opening Times: Matchdays only
Telephone Nº: (01307) 463576

GROUND INFORMATION
Away Supporters' Entrances & Sections:
West End entrances for West End Terracing and North part of the Main Stand

ADMISSION INFO (2024/2025 PRICES)
Adult Standing: £15.00   Adult Seating: £17.00
Senior Citizen Standing: £8.00   Seating: £10.00
Under-17s Standing/Seating: £6.00

DISABLED INFORMATION
Wheelchairs: 5 spaces each for home and away fans accommodated to the west of the Main Stand
Helpers: Admitted
Prices: Normal prices for disabled fans. Free for helpers
Disabled Toilets: Available in the Hospitality Suite and the South West corner of the stadium
Contact: (01307) 464142 (Bookings are necessary) – Iain Reid (Disability Officer)

Travelling Supporters' Information:
Routes: Take the A85/M90 to Dundee and then the A929. Exit at the 2nd turn-off (signposted for Forfar). On the outskirts of Forfar, turn right at the T-junction and then left at the next major road. The ground is signposted on the left (down the cobbled street with the railway arch).

PETERHEAD FC

Founded: 1891   (**Entered League**: 2000)
Nickname: 'Blue Toon'
Ground: Balmoor Stadium, Peterhead   AB42 1EQ
Ground Capacity: 4,000
Seating Capacity: 1,000
Record Attendance: 4,855 (vs Rangers, 2013)

Colours: Royal Blue Shirts, Shorts are Royal Blue with White piping
Telephone Nº: (01779) 478256
Website: www.peterheadfc.co.uk
E-mail: office@peterheadfc.co.uk

GENERAL INFORMATION
Car Parking: At the ground
Coach Parking: At the ground
Nearest Railway Station: Aberdeen
Nearest Bus Station: Peterhead
Club Shop: At the ground
Opening Times: Monday to Friday plus Saturday matchdays 9.00am to 5.00pm
Telephone Nº: (01779) 478256

GROUND INFORMATION
Away Supporters' Entrances & Sections:
Segregation only used when required which is very rare

ADMISSION INFO (2024/2025 PRICES)
Adult Standing: £15.00
Adult Seating: £17.00
Child/Concessionary Standing: £8.00
Child/Concessionary Seating: £10.00
Note: Under-13s stand for free or pay just £2.00 for seating when accompanied by a paying adult.

DISABLED INFORMATION
Wheelchairs: Accommodated in the Main Stand
Helpers: Admitted
Prices: Concessionary prices for disabled fans in wheelchairs. Free of charge for helpers.
Disabled Toilets: Available in the Main Stand
Contact: (01779) 478256   (Bookings are necessary) Nat Porter (Disability Officer)

Travelling Supporters' Information:
Routes: The ground is situated on the left of the main road from Fraserburgh (A952), 300 yards past the swimming pool.

STIRLING ALBION FC

Founded: 1945 (**Entered League**: 1946)
Nickname: 'The Binos'
Ground: Forthbank Stadium, Springkerse Roundabout, Stirling, FK7 7UJ
Ground Capacity: 3,808
Seating Capacity: 2,508
Record Attendance: 3,808 (17th February 1996)

Colours: Shirts are Red with White sleeves, Red Shorts
Telephone Nº: (01786) 450399
Ticket Office: (01786) 450399
Website: www.stirlingalbionfc.co.uk
E-mail: office@stirlingalbionfc.co.uk

GENERAL INFORMATION
Car Parking: At the ground and Springkerse Retail Park (5 to 10 minutes walk)
Coach Parking: Adjacent to the ground
Nearest Railway Station: Stirling (2 miles)
Nearest Bus Station: Stirling (2 miles)
Club Shop: At the ground
Opening Times: Weekdays and Saturday Matchdays. Please contact the club for further information.
Telephone Nº: (01786) 450399

GROUND INFORMATION
Away Supporters' Entrances & Sections:
South Terracing and East Stand

ADMISSION INFO (2024/2025 PRICES)
Adult Standing/Seating: £17.00
Concessionary Standing/Seating: £12.00
Under-18s Standing/Seating: £8.00
Note: Under-12s are admitted free of charge when accompanied by a paying adult.

DISABLED INFORMATION
Wheelchairs: 18 spaces each for home and away fans
Helpers: Admitted
Prices: Free of charge for disabled fans in wheelchairs. Helpers for fans in wheelchairs are admitted free of charge
Disabled Toilets: 2 available beneath each stand
Contact: (01786) 450399 (Bookings are necessary) – Stevie Peebles (Disability Officer): office@stirlingalbionfc.co.uk

Travelling Supporters' Information:
Routes: Follow signs for Stirling from the M9/M80 Northbound. From Pirnhall Roundabout follow signs for Alloa/St. Andrew's to the 4th roundabout and then turn left for the stadium.

STRANRAER FC

Founded: 1870 (**Entered League**: 1955)
Nickname: 'The Blues'
Ground: Stair Park, London Road, Stranraer, DG9 8BS
Ground Capacity: 4,178
Seating Capacity: 1,830
Record Attendance: 6,500 (24th January 1948)

Colours: Blue shirts with White shorts
Telephone N°: (01776) 703271
Ticket Office: (01776) 703271
Website: www.stranraerfc.org
E-mail: secretary@stranraerfc.org

GENERAL INFORMATION
Car Parking: Car Park at the ground
Coach Parking: Port Rodie, Stranraer
Nearest Railway Station: Stranraer (1 mile)
Nearest Bus Station: Port Rodie, Stranraer
Club Shop: At the ground
Opening Times: Matchdays only from 2.15pm to 3.00pm and also during half-time
Telephone N°: None

GROUND INFORMATION
Away Supporters' Entrances & Sections:
London Road entrances for the 'Coo Shed' (North Stand)

ADMISSION INFO (2024/2025 PRICES)
Adult Standing/Seating: £15.00
Senior Citizen Standing/Seating: £10.00
Under-16s Standing/Seating: £5.00
Note: Under-5s are admitted free with a paying adult

DISABLED INFORMATION
Wheelchairs: 6 spaces each for Home and Away fans in front of the Main Stand
Helpers: Please phone the club for details
Prices: Please phone the club for details
Disabled Toilets: Available in the Main Stand
Contact: (01776) 703271 (Bookings are necessary) – Hilde Law (Disability Officer): secretary@stranraerfc.org

Travelling Supporters' Information:
Routes: From the West: Take the A75 to Stranraer and the ground is on the left-hand side of the road in a public park shortly after entering the town; From the North: Take the A77 and follow it to where it joins with the A75 (then as West). The ground is set back from the road and the floodlights are clearly visible.

THE SPARTANS FC

Founded: 1951
Nickname: None
Ground: The Spartans Community Football Academy, Ainslie Park Stadium, 94 Pilton Drive, Edinburgh, EH5 2HF
Telephone Nº: (0131) 552 7854

Ground Capacity: 8,500
Seating Capacity: 534
Record Attendance: 3,127 (vs Man United XI in 2011)
Colours: White shirts with Red shorts and White socks
Website: www.spartansfc.com
E-mail: macabiteam@hotmail.com

GENERAL INFORMATION
Car Parking: At the ground
Coach Parking: At the ground by prior arrangement
Nearest Railway Station: Edinburgh Waverley (2¾ miles)
Nearest Bus Station: St. Andrew's Square
Club Shop: At the ground

GROUND INFORMATION
Away Supporters' Entrances & Sections:
No usual segregation. Enter through Ainslie Park Leisure Centre car park

ADMISSION INFO (2024/2025 PRICES)
Adult Standing/Seating: £17.00
Ages 12 to 16 Standing/Seating: £5.00
Concessionary Standing/Seating: £12.00
Note: Under-12s are admitted free with a paying adult

DISABLED INFORMATION
Wheelchairs: Accommodated in Main Stand and Terraces
Helpers: Admitted
Prices: Concessionary prices are charged for disabled fans. Helpers are admitted free of charge
Disabled Toilets: Available
Contact: (0131) 552-7854 (Bookings are not necessary) – Gary Betts (Disability Officer): garrybetts@spartanscfa.com

Travelling Supporters' Information:
Routes: From the West: Take the A90 Queensferry Road into Edinburgh and continue until reaching the A902 (Telford Road). Turn left into Telford Road and take the 3rd exit at the roundabout into Ferry Road. Turn left into Pilton Drive immediately after passing the Morrisons Supermarket and enter the ground through Ainslie Park leisure centre; From the East: Take the A1 into Edinburgh and at the 1st roundabout take the 2nd exit into Milton Link and continue onto Sir Harry Lauder Road (A199). Continue along the A199 for approximately 2½ miles past Leith then turn left onto the A902 which continues into Ferry Road. Turn Pilton Drive just before the Morrisons Supermarket, then as above.

THE HIGHLAND FOOTBALL LEAGUE

Founded 1893

Secretary Mr John Campbell

Website www.highlandfootballleague.com

Clubs for the 2024-2025 Season

Banks O'Dee FC .... Page 50
Brechin City FC .... Page 51
Brora Rangers FC .... Page 52
Buckie Thistle FC .... Page 53
Clachnacuddin FC .... Page 54
Deveronvale FC .... Page 55
Formartine United FC .... Page 56
Forres Mechanics FC .... Page 57
Fraserburgh FC .... Page 58
Huntly FC .... Page 59
Inverurie Loco Works FC .... Page 60
Keith FC .... Page 61
Lossiemouth FC .... Page 62
Nairn County FC .... Page 63
Rothes FC .... Page 64
Strathspey Thistle FC .... Page 65
Turriff United FC .... Page 66
Wick Academy FC .... Page 67

BANKS O'DEE FC

Founded: 1902
Nickname: 'The Rechabites' or 'The Dee'
Ground: Spain Park, Abbotswell Road, Aberdeen, AB12 3AB
Ground Capacity: 876
Seating Capacity: 100

Colours: Dark & Light Blue Hooped shirts with White shorts
Contact Phone N°: None
Website: www.banksodeefc.com

GENERAL INFORMATION
Car Parking: At the ground
Coach Parking: At the ground
Nearest Railway Station: Aberdeen
Club Shop: Sales via the club's website

GROUND INFORMATION
Away Supporters' Entrances & Sections: No usual segregation

ADMISSION INFO (2024/2025 PRICES)
Adult Standing/Seating: £10.00
Concessionary Standing/Seating: £5.00
Note: Under-12s are admitted free with a paying adult

DISABLED INFORMATION
Wheelchairs: Accommodated in the stand
Helpers: Admitted
Prices: Free of charge for fans with disabilities. Helpers are charged half the usual matchday admission price
Disabled Toilets: available
Contact: 07974 737043   (Bookings are not necessary)

Travelling Supporters' Information:
Routes: From all locations: Spain Park is located South of the River Dee near the Abbotswell area of the city, so take the A90 to the junction with the A956 then follow that road into Aberdeen passing the Alten & East Tullos Industrial Estates on the right. Continue along and after passing Lidl on the right turn left at the traffic lights into Abbotswell Rd & Spain Park is then located near the Banks O'Dee Sports Club on the right.

BRECHIN CITY FC

Founded: 1906 (**Entered League**: 1923)
Nickname: 'The City'
Ground: Glebe Park, Trinity Road, Brechin, Angus, DD9 6BJ
Ground Capacity: 4,123
Seating Capacity: 1,528
Record Attendance: 8,122 (3rd February 1973)

Colours: Red shirts with Black shorts
Telephone Nº: (01356) 623344
Ticket Office: (01356) 623344
Website: www.brechincity.com
E-mail: secretary@brechincity.com

GENERAL INFORMATION
Car Parking: Small Car Park at the ground and street parking
Coach Parking: Street parking
Nearest Railway Station: Montrose (8 miles)
Nearest Bus Station: Brechin
Club Shop: At the ground
Opening Times: Matchdays Only from 1.00pm until kick-off and then after the game until 8.00pm.
Telephone Nº: (01356) 622856

GROUND INFORMATION
Away Supporters' Entrances & Sections:
Enter from the Trinity Road end for the David H Will Stand and the Hedge Side

ADMISSION INFO (2024/2025 PRICES)
Adult Standing: £10.00
Adult Seating: £12.00
Concessionary Standing: £5.00
Concessionary Seating: £7.00
Under-16s: Free but must make application.

DISABLED INFORMATION
Wheelchairs: 44 spaces are available in total
Helpers: Admitted
Prices: Free of charge for both disabled fans and helpers
Disabled Toilets: Two available in the Covered Enclosure
Contact: (01356) 622856 (Bookings are not necessary) – David Dewar (Disability Officer): dlo@brechincityfc.com

Travelling Supporters' Information:
Routes: From the South and West: Take the M90 to the A94 and continue along past the first 'Brechin' turn-off. Take the second turn signposted 'Brechin'. On entering Brechin, the ground is on the left-hand side of the road between some houses.

BRORA RANGERS FC

Founded: 1878
Nickname: 'The Cattachs'
Ground: Dudgeon Park, 14 Seaforth Place, Brora, KW9 6PL
Ground Capacity: 4,000
Seating Capacity: 200
Record Attendance: 2,000 (31st August 1963)

Colours: Red shirts and shorts
Correspondence Address: Kevin Mackay, 2 Muirfield Road, Brora KW9 6QP
Website: brorarangers.football
E-mail: brorarangersfc@highlandleague.com

GENERAL INFORMATION
Car Parking: Adjacent to the ground
Coach Parking: Adjacent to the ground
Nearest Railway Station: Brora
Nearest Bus Station: Brora
Club Shop: At the ground
Opening Times: Matchdays only
Telephone Nº: (01408) 621231

GROUND INFORMATION
Away Supporters' Entrances & Sections:
No usual segregation

ADMISSION INFO (2024/2025 PRICES)
Adult Standing: £10.00
Adult Seating: £12.00
Concession Standing: £5.00
Concession Seating: £7.00

DISABLED INFORMATION
Wheelchairs: Accommodated
Helpers: Admitted
Prices: Free of charge for fans with disabilities and helpers
Disabled Toilets: Please check with club
Contact: (01408) 621231 (Bookings are necessary)

Travelling Supporters' Information:
Routes: Take the A9 Northbound from Inverness and the Stadium is situated on the right upon entering the town. It is clearly visible from the road.

BUCKIE THISTLE FC

Founded: 1889
Former Names: None
Nickname: 'The Jags'
Ground: Victoria Park, Midmar Street, Buckie, AB56 1BJ
Record Attendance: 8,168 (vs Falkirk, 1/3/1958)
Ground Capacity: 5,000
Seating Capacity: 400

Colours: Green and White hooped shirts, White shorts
Correspondence: c/o David Pirie, St. Aethans, 33 Station Road, Findochty AB56 4PJ
Telephone Nº: (01542) 831946
Website: www.buckiethistlefc.co.uk
E-mail: buckiethistlefc@highlandleague.com

GENERAL INFORMATION
Car Parking: Adjacent to the ground
Coach Parking: Adjacent to the ground
Nearest Railway Station: Keith (12 miles)
Nearest Bus Station: Buckie
Club Shop: In the Supporters' Club inside the ground
Social Club: Victoria Park Function Hall at the ground
Social Club Telephone Nº: (01542) 831454

GROUND INFORMATION
Away Supporters' Entrances & Sections:
No usual segregation

ADMISSION INFO (2024/2025 PRICES)
Adult Standing/Seating: £10.00
Concessionary Standing/Seating: £5.00
Note: Under-12s are admitted free with a paying adult

DISABLED INFORMATION
Wheelchairs: Accommodated in front of the stand
Helpers: Admitted
Prices: Concessionary prices apply
Disabled Toilets: Available in the Victoria Park Function Hall
Contact: (0797 6762367) (Bookings are helpful)

Travelling Supporters' Information:
Routes: From the East and West: Exit the A98 onto the A942 towards Buckie. Go straight on at the roundabout and travel along Buckie High Street. Turn left at the roundabout next to Cluny Square into West Church Street then take the 1st left into South Pringle Street. The ground is straight ahead.

CLACHNACUDDIN FC

Founded: 1886
Nickname: 'Lilywhites'
Ground: Grant Street Park, Wyvis Place, Inverness, IV3 8DR
Ground Capacity: 3,000
Seating Capacity: 154

Record Attendance: 9,000 (27th August 1951)
Colours: White shirts with Black shorts
Website: www.clachfc.co.uk
E-mail: info@clachfc.co.uk

GENERAL INFORMATION
Car Parking: Adjacent to the ground
Coach Parking: Adjacent to the ground
Nearest Railway Station: Inverness
Nearest Bus Station: Inverness
Club Shop: At the ground
Opening Times: Matchdays only

GROUND INFORMATION
Away Supporters' Entrances & Sections:
No usual segregation

ADMISSION INFO (2024/2025 PRICES)
Adult Standing: £10.00
Adult Seating: £11.00
Child/Concession Standing: £5.00
Child/Concession Seating: £6.00

DISABLED INFORMATION
Wheelchairs: Accommodated
Helpers: Admitted
Prices: £4.00 for disabled fans. Helpers admitted free
Disabled Toilets: Available
Contact: Via the E-mail address shown above
(Bookings are not necessary)

Travelling Supporters' Information:
Routes: From the East and South: From the roundabout at the junction of the A9 and A96, proceed into the Town Centre and over the River Ness. Turn right at the traffic lights (onto the A862 to Dingwall), go up Kenneth Street and over the roundabout onto Telford Street for 200 yards before turning right into Telford Road opposite the Fish Shop. At the top, turn left onto Lower Kessack Street and left again. Finally, turn left into Wyvis Place and the ground is on the left.

DEVERONVALE FC

Founded: 1938
Nickname: 'The Vale'
Ground: Princess Royal Park, 56 Airlie Gardens, Banff AB45 1AZ
Ground Capacity: 2,651
Seating Capacity: 360
Record Attendance: 5,000 (27th April 1952)

Colours: Shirts are Red with White trim, Red shorts
Telephone Nº: (01261) 818303
Contact Address: Stewart McPherson, 8 Victoria Place, Banff AB45 1EL
Contact Phone Nº: (01261) 818303
Website: www.deveronvale.co.uk
E-mail: info@deveronvale.co.uk

GENERAL INFORMATION
Car Parking: Adjacent to the ground plus street parking.
Coach Parking: Bridge Road Car Park
Nearest Railway Station: Keith (20 miles)
Nearest Bus Station: Macduff (1 mile)
Club Shop: At the ground
Opening Times: Matchdays only
Telephone Nº: (01261) 818303

GROUND INFORMATION
Away Supporters' Entrances & Sections: No usual segregation

ADMISSION INFO (2024/2025 PRICES)
Adult Standing: £12.00
Adult Seating: £14.00
Concessionary Standing: £6.00
Concessionary Seating: £8.00
Note: Under-12s are admitted free with a paying adult

DISABLED INFORMATION
Wheelchairs: Accommodated
Helpers: Admitted
Prices: Concessionary prices for the disabled and carers
Disabled Toilets: Available
Contact: (01261) 818303 (Bookings are necessary)

Travelling Supporters' Information:
Routes: From Aberdeen: Enter the town at Banff Bridge – the ground is situated ¼ mile along on the right; From Inverness: Travel through Banff on the main bypass and the ground is situated on the left, ¼ mile before Banff Bridge.

FORMARTINE UNITED FC

Founded: 1948
Nickname: 'United'
Ground: North Lodge Park, Old Meldrum Road, Pitmedden   AB41 7PA
Ground Capacity: 2,500
Seating Capacity: 300

Record Attendance: 1,500
Colours: Red & White striped shirts with Red shorts
Contact Phone N°:   07738 468267
Website: www.formartineunitedfc.co.uk

GENERAL INFORMATION
Car Parking: At the ground
Coach Parking: At the ground
Nearest Railway Station: Inverurie (11 miles)
Nearest Bus Station: Inverurie
Club Shop: At the ground
Opening Times: Matchdays only

GROUND INFORMATION
Away Supporters' Entrances & Sections:
No usual segregation

ADMISSION INFO (2024/2025 PRICES)
Adult Standing: £10.00
Adult Seating: £10.00
Concessionary Standing/Seating: £5.00
Under-12s Standing/Seating: £5.00

DISABLED INFORMATION
Wheelchairs: Accommodated
Helpers: Admitted with prior notice
Prices: Normal prices apply for the disabled and helpers
Disabled Toilets: Available
Contact: 07738 468267

Travelling Supporters' Information:
Routes: Pitmedden is located approximately 15 miles north of Aberdeen on the A920 between Oldmeldrum and Ellon. North Lodge Park is situated just to the west of Pitmedden by the junction of the A920 and the B9000 which heads into Pitmedden itself.

FORRES MECHANICS FC

Founded: 1884
Nickname: 'The Mighty Cans'
Ground: Mosset Park, Lea Road, Forres IV36 1AU
Ground Capacity: 2,700
Seating Capacity: 502
Record Attendance: 7,000 (2nd February 1957)

Colours: Maroon & Gold shirts with Gold shorts
Telephone Nº: (01309) 675096
Website: www.forresmechanics.net
Email: forresmechanicsfc@highlandfootballleague.com

GENERAL INFORMATION
Car Parking: At the ground
Coach Parking: At the ground
Nearest Railway Station: Forres
Nearest Bus Station: Forres
Club Shop: At the ground
Opening Times: Matchdays only
Telephone Nº: (01309) 675096

GROUND INFORMATION
Away Supporters' Entrances & Sections:
No usual segregation

ADMISSION INFO (2024/2025 PRICES)
Adult Standing: £10.00
Adult Seating: £12.00
Child/Senior Citizen Standing: £6.00
Child/Senior Citizen Seating: £8.00
Note: Under-12s are admitted free with a paying adult

DISABLED INFORMATION
Wheelchairs: Accommodated
Prices: Free of charge for fans with disabilities. Helpers are charged half the usual matchday admission price
Disabled Toilets: One available
Contact: (01309) 675096 (Bookings are not necessary)

Travelling Supporters' Information:
Routes: From A96 East (Inverness): Turn off the A96 onto the B9011. Continue along this road and pass Tesco, turn left at the roundabout then immediately right into Invererne Road. Follow for about ½ mile then turn right across Lea Bridge then left for the ground; From A96 West (Aberdeen): Drive into Forres on the A96 passing the ground on your left. After a short distance, turn left onto the A940 (Market Street). Immediately before the roundabout turn left into Invererne Road. Then as above.

FRASERBURGH FC

Founded: 1910
Nickname: 'The Broch'
Ground: Bellslea Park, Seaforth Street, Fraserburgh, AB43 9BB
Ground Capacity: 1,865
Seating Capacity: 300
Record Attendance: 5,800 (13th February 1954)

Colours: Black and White striped shirts, Black shorts
Telephone Nº: (01346) 518444
Contact Address: Finlay Noble, 18 Bawdley Head, Fraserburgh AB43 9SE
Contact Phone Nº: (01346) 518444
Mobile Phone Contact Nº: 07852 178634
Website: www.thebroch.online
E-mail: finlay.noble@fraserburghfc.co.uk

GENERAL INFORMATION
Car Parking: At the ground
Coach Parking: At the ground
Nearest Railway Station: Aberdeen (40 miles)
Nearest Bus Station: Fraserburgh
Club Shop: Designs On You, 46 Mid Street, Fraserburgh
Opening Times: Monday to Saturday 9.00am to 5.00pm
Telephone Nº: (01346) 378958

GROUND INFORMATION
Away Supporters' Entrances & Sections:
No usual segregation

ADMISSION INFO (2024/2025 PRICES)
Adult Standing: £10.00
Adult Seating: £10.00
Child Standing: £5.00
Child Seating: £5.00
Note: Under-14s are admitted free with a paying adult

DISABLED INFORMATION
Wheelchairs: Accommodated
Helpers: Admitted
Prices: Normal prices apply
Disabled Toilets: Available
Contact: (01346) 518444 or Jason Nicol 07540 497105
(Prior bookings would be appreciated)

Travelling Supporters' Information:
Routes: The ground is situated in the Town Centre, off Seaforth Street.

HUNTLY FC

Founded: 1928
Nickname: None
Ground: Safelift Christie Park, East Park Street, Huntly, Aberdeenshire AB54 8JE
Ground Capacity: 2,200
Seating Capacity: 270
Record Attendance: 4,500 (18th February 1995)

Colours: Black and Gold shirts with Black shorts
Telephone Nº: (01466) 793548
Social Club Phone Nº: (01466) 793680
Matchday Contact: Grant Turner – 07989 131492
grant.turner@huntlyfc.co.uk
Non-Matchday Contact Nº: 07867625303
Website: www.huntlyfc.co.uk

GENERAL INFORMATION
Car Parking: At the ground
Coach Parking: At the ground
Nearest Railway Station: Huntly (1 mile)
Nearest Bus Station: Huntly (¼ mile)
Club Shop: At the ground
Opening Times: Matchdays only

GROUND INFORMATION
Away Supporters' Entrances & Sections: No usual segregation

ADMISSION INFO (2024/2025 PRICES)
Adult Standing: £10.00
Adult Seating: £12.00
Child/Concessionary Standing: £5.00
Child/Concessionary Seating: £7.00
Note: Up to two Under-14s are admitted free with a paying adult

DISABLED INFORMATION
Wheelchairs: Accommodated
Helpers: Please contact the club for details
Prices: Please contact the club for details
Disabled Toilets: Available
Contact: (01466) 793269 (Bookings are not necessary)

Travelling Supporters' Information:
Routes: Enter Town off the A96 and proceed along King George V Avenue and Gordon Street. Pass through the Town Centre Square, along Castle Street to East Park Street and the ground is on the right before the Castle.

INVERURIE LOCO WORKS FC

Founded: 1902
Nickname: 'Locos'
Ground: Harlaw Park, Harlaw Road, Inverurie, AB51 4SF
Ground Capacity: 2,500
Seating Capacity: 250

Record Attendance: 2,250
Colours: Red and Black shirts, Black shorts
Telephone Nº: (01467) 622168
Website: www.inverurielocos.com
E-mail: inverurielocoworksfc@highlandleague.com

GENERAL INFORMATION
Car Parking: At the ground
Coach Parking: At the ground
Nearest Railway Station: Inverurie
Nearest Bus Station: Inverurie
Club Shop: Merchandise available on matchdays and via inverurie-loco-works.footballkit.co.uk

GROUND INFORMATION
Away Supporters' Entrances & Sections: No usual segregation

ADMISSION INFO (2024/2025 PRICES)
Adult Standing: £10.00
Adult Seating: £11.00
Child/Senior Citizen Standing: £5.00
Child/Senior Citizen Seating: £6.00
Note: Under-14s are admitted free with a paying adult

DISABLED INFORMATION
Wheelchairs: Accommodated in the Covered Enclosure
Helpers: Admitted
Prices: Concessionary prices are charged for disabled fans. Helpers are admitted free of charge
Disabled Toilets: Available

Travelling Supporters' Information:
Routes: From the North: Take the A96 to the Inverurie bypass then turn left at the Morrisons roundabout along Blackhall Road and left at the next roundabout into Boroughmuir Drive. Cross the next roundabout and then turn 1st right into Hawlaw Road for the ground; From the South: Take the A96 to the Inverurie bypass then as above.

KEITH FC

Founded: 1910
Nickname: 'Maroons'
Ground: Kynoch Park, Balloch Road, Keith AB55 5EN
Ground Capacity: 4,000
Seating Capacity: 370
Record Attendance: 5,820 (4th February 1928)

Colours: Shirts and shorts are Maroon with White trim
Telephone Nº: (01542) 888038
Website: www.keithfc.com
E-mail: keithfc@highlandleague.com

GENERAL INFORMATION
Car Parking: Street parking in Balloch Road, Moss Street and Reidhaven Square
Coach Parking: Balloch Road or Bridge Street Coach Park
Nearest Railway Station: Keith (1 mile)
Nearest Bus Station: Keith
Club Shop: At the ground
Opening Times: Wednesday to Thursday 9.00am to 4.00pm and Friday 9.00am to 12.30pm.
Telephone Nº: (01542) 888038

GROUND INFORMATION
Away Supporters' Entrances & Sections:
No usual segregation except for some Cup Ties

ADMISSION INFO (2024/2025 PRICES)
Adult Standing: £10.00
Adult Seating: £11.00
Child Standing: £5.00
Child Seating: £6.00
Note: Under-14s are admitted free with a paying adult

DISABLED INFORMATION
Wheelchairs: Accommodated
Helpers: Admitted
Prices: Free of charge for both disabled fans in wheelchairs and their helpers
Disabled Toilets: Available
Contact: (01542) 888038

Travelling Supporters' Information:
Routes: From Inverness: Follow the A96 through Keith before turning left opposite the newsagents and public toilets in Reidhaven Square. Follow signs for the Moray College Learning Centre, take the next left into Balloch Road and the ground is on the right; From Aberdeen: After Entering Keith turn right opposite the newsagents in Reidhaven Square. Then as above.

LOSSIEMOUTH FC

Founded: 1945
Nickname: 'Coasters'
Ground: Grant Park, Kellas Avenue, Lossiemouth IV31 6JG
Ground Capacity: 2,400
Seating Capacity: 150
Record Attendance: 2,800 (28th December 1948)

Colours: Red shirts and shorts
Telephone Nº: (01343) 813717
Social Club Nº: (01343) 813168
Contact Address: Alan McIntosh, 3 Forties Place, Lossiemouth IV31 6SS
Contact Phone Nº: (01343) 813328 & (07890) 749053
Website: www.lossiemouthfc.co.uk
E-mail: lossiemouthfconline@hotmail.com

GENERAL INFORMATION
Car Parking: At the ground
Coach Parking: At the ground
Nearest Railway Station: Elgin
Nearest Bus Station: Lossiemouth
Club Shop: At the ground
Opening Times: Matchdays only
Telephone Nº: (01343) 813168

GROUND INFORMATION
Away Supporters' Entrances & Sections:
No usual segregation

ADMISSION INFO (2024/2025 PRICES)
Adult Standing: £10.00
Adult Seating: £11.00
Concessionary Standing: £5.00
Concessionary Seating: £6.00
Note: Under-14s are admitted free with a paying adult

DISABLED INFORMATION
Wheelchairs: Accommodated
Helpers: Admitted
Prices: Concessionary prices apply
Disabled Toilets: Available
Contact: (01343) 813328 (Alan McIntosh) (Please book)

Travelling Supporters' Information:
Routes: Take the A941 to Lossiemouth. As you enter the town take the 3rd turning on the right into Moray Street. Continue along Moray Street then take the 4th turning on the right into Kellas Avenue. Grant Park is at the end of this road.

NAIRN COUNTY FC

Founded: 1914
Nickname: 'The Wee County'
Ground: Station Park, Balblair Road, Nairn IV12 5LT
Ground Capacity: 3,000
Seating Capacity: 250
Record Attendance: 4,000 (2nd September 1950)

Colours: Yellow and Black Shirts, Black shorts
Telephone Nº: (01667) 454298
Contact Address: Ian Finlayson, 2 Chattan Drive, Nairn IV12 4QR
Contact Phone Nº: 07821 828852
Website: www.nairncountyfc.co.uk
E-mail: info@nairncountyfc.co.uk

GENERAL INFORMATION
Car Parking: Limited number of spaces adjoining the ground
Coach Parking: At the ground
Nearest Railway Station: Nairn (adjacent)
Nearest Bus Station: King Street, Nairn (½ mile)
Club Shop: At the ground
Opening Times: Matchdays only

GROUND INFORMATION
Away Supporters' Entrances & Sections:
No usual segregation

ADMISSION INFO (2024/2025 PRICES)
Adult Standing: £10.00
Adult Seating: £11.00
Senior Citizen/Child Standing: £5.00
Senior Citizen/Child Seating: £6.00
Note: Under-13s are admitted free with a paying adult

DISABLED INFORMATION
Wheelchairs: Accommodated in the Stand
Prices: Free of charge for fans with disabilities. Helpers are charged half the usual matchday admission price
Disabled Toilets: Available
Contact: Ian Finlayson (Disability Officer): ifinl@hotmail.com 07821 828852 (Bookings are appreciated)

Travelling Supporters' Information:
Routes: The ground is situated on the south side of Nairn at Balblair Road, adjacent to the Railway Station.

ROTHES FC

Founded: 1938
Former Names: Rothes Victoria FC
Nickname: 'The Speysiders'
Ground: Mackessack Park, Station Street, Rothes, AB38 7BY
Ground Capacity: 1,731
Seating Capacity: 167

Record Attendance: 2,054 (September 1946)
Colours: Tangerine shirts with Black shorts
Contact Telephone N°: 07876343957
Social Club N°: (01340) 831248
Website: www.rothesfc.co.uk
E-mail: rothesfcinfo@gmail.com

GENERAL INFORMATION
Car Parking: At the ground
Coach Parking: At the ground
Nearest Railway Station: Elgin
Nearest Bus Station: Elgin (36 Bus Service)
Club Shop: At the ground during home matches and also via the club's website.

GROUND INFORMATION
Away Supporters' Entrances & Sections:
No usual segregation

ADMISSION INFO (2024/2025 PRICES)
Adult Standing: £10.00
Adult Seating: £12.00
Concessionary Standing: £5.00
Concessionary Seating: £7.00
Note: Under-14s are admitted free with a paying adult

DISABLED INFORMATION
Wheelchairs: Accommodated
Helpers: Admitted
Prices: Normal prices for the disabled. Helpers admitted free
Disabled Toilets: Available

Travelling Supporters' Information:
Routes: From the A96 take the A941 signposted for Perth and follow into Rothes. After entering the town take the 2nd exit (A941 Perth) before immediately turning 1st left down a small track. Follow this past the distillery to reach the ground.

STRATHSPEY THISTLE FC

Founded: 1993
Former Names: None
Nickname: 'Thistle' 'The Strathy Jags'
Ground: Seafield Park, Heathfield Road, Grantown-on-Spey PH26 3HY
Ground Capacity: 1,600
Seating Capacity: 150

Colours: Blue shirts and shorts
Ground Telephone Nº: (01479) 873344
Contact Address: Clive Wolstenholme (Secretary), 18 Munro Place, Aviemore PH22 1TE
Contact Nº: 07837 917746
Website: www.strathspeythistlefc.com

GENERAL INFORMATION
Car Parking: At the ground and nearby
Coach Parking: At the ground
Nearest Railway Station: Aviemore (14 miles)
Club Shop: None

GROUND INFORMATION
Away Supporters' Entrances & Sections:
No usual segregation

ADMISSION INFO (2024/2025 PRICES)
Adult Standing: £10.00
Adult Seating: £10.00
Senior Citizen/Under-16s Standing/Seating: £5.00
Note: Under-12s are admitted free with a paying adult

DISABLED INFORMATION
Wheelchairs: Accommodated in the stand
Helpers: Admitted
Prices: Concessionary prices apply
Disabled Toilets: Available
Contact: (01479) 873344 (Bookings are not necessary)

Travelling Supporters' Information:
Routes: From Forres: Take the A939 to Grantown-on-Spey and upon entering town, take the 1st left then the 1st right into Heathfield Road. Continue along then turn 1st left into Golf Course Road and the ground is ¼ mile along the road.
From Aviemore: Take the A939 to Grantown-on-Spey and turn right at the first set of traffic lights into Woodside Avenue. Continue along the road for about ½ mile then turn right into Golf Course Road for the ground.

TURRIFF UNITED FC

Founded: 1954
Former Names: None
Nickname: 'Turra' or 'United'
Ground: The Haughs, Queens Road, Turriff, AB53 4ER
Ground Capacity: 2,135
Seating Capacity: 135
Record Attendance: 1,791 (vs Hibernian, 2016)

Colours: Navy Blue shirts and shorts
Telephone N°: (01888) 562169
Contact Address: Philip Napier, Seventh Lodge, Fyvie Castle, Fyvie AB53 8JS
Website: www.turriffunited.co.uk
E-mail: turriffunitedfc@highlandleague.com

GENERAL INFORMATION
Car Parking: At the ground
Coach Parking: At the ground
Nearest Railway Station: Inverurie (20 miles)
Nearest Bus Station: Turriff
Club Shop: None

GROUND INFORMATION
Away Supporters' Entrances & Sections:
No usual segregation

ADMISSION INFO (2024/2025 PRICES)
Adult Standing: £10.00
Adult Seating: £11.00
Child Standing: £5.00
Child Seating: £6.00
Note: Under-14s are admitted free with a paying adult

DISABLED INFORMATION
Wheelchairs: Accommodated
Helpers: Admitted
Prices: Free of charge for both the disabled and helpers
Disabled Toilets: Available
Contact: 07928 367286 (Bookings are necessary)

Travelling Supporters' Information:
Routes: From the North: Take the A947 to Turriff and, after the only roundabout in town, turn 1st right down to The Haughs. The ground is adjacent to the Swimming Pool.

WICK ACADEMY FC

Founded: 1893
Nickname: 'The Scorries'
Ground: Harmsworth Park, South Road, Wick, Caithness KW1 5NH
Ground Capacity: 2,412
Seating Capacity: 102
Record Attendance: 2,400 (vs Hearts, 30th July 1984)

Colours: Black and White striped shirts, Black shorts
Telephone Nº: 07803 667598
Contact Address: Melanie Roger, 7 Thorfinn Place, Thurso KW14 7LN
Contact Nº: 07803 667593
Website: www.wick-academy.co.uk
E-mail: wickacademy@highlandleague.com

GENERAL INFORMATION
Car Parking: At the ground
Coach Parking: At the ground
Nearest Railway Station: Wick (10 minutes walk)
Nearest Bus Station: Wick
Club Shop: Please contact the club for details
Telephone Nº: (01955) 602446

GROUND INFORMATION
Away Supporters' Entrances & Sections:
No usual segregation

ADMISSION INFO (2024/2025 PRICES)
Adult Standing: £10.00
Adult Seating: £10.00
Ages 12-16/Senior Citizen Standing: £5.00
Ages 12-16/Senior Citizen Seating: £5.00
Note: Under-12s are admitted free with a paying adult

DISABLED INFORMATION
Wheelchairs: 2 spaces available in the North Stand
Prices: Free of charge for fans with disabilities. Helpers are charged half the usual matchday admission price
Disabled Toilets: Available
Contact: 07803667598 (Bookings are necessary)

Travelling Supporters' Information:
Routes: The ground is situated on the A99 road from Inverness beside the Cemetery.

The Scottish Lowland Football League

Founded 2013

Website www.slfl.co.uk

Clubs for the 2024-2025 Season

Albion Rovers FC .... Page 69

Berwick Rangers FC .... Page 70

Bo'ness United FC .... Page 71

Broomhill FC .... Page 72

Broxburn Athletic FC .... Page 73

Caledonian Braves FC .... Page 74

Celtic 'B' FC .... Page 75

Civil Service Stollers FC .... Page 76

Cowdenbeath FC .... Page 77

Cumbernauld Colts FC .... Page 78

East Kilbride FC .... Page 79

East Stirlingshire FC .... Page 80

Gala Fairydean Rovers FC .... Page 81

Gretna 2008 FC .... Page 82

Hearts 'B' FC .... Page 83

Linlithgow Rose FC .... Page 84

Tranent Juniors FC .... Page 85

University of Stirling FC .... Page 86

ALBION ROVERS FC

Founded: 1882
Nickname: 'Wee Rovers'
Ground: The Reigart Stadium, Main Street, Coatbridge, Lanarkshire ML5 3RB
Ground Capacity: 1,238
Seating Capacity: 489
Record Attendance: 27,381 (8th February 1936)

Colours: Red and Yellow shirts with Red shorts
Telephone Nº: (01236) 606334
Ticket Office: (01236) 606334
Website: www.albionroversfc.com
E-mail: secretary@albionroversfc.com

GENERAL INFORMATION
Car Parking: Street parking and Albion Street
Coach Parking: Street parking only
Nearest Railway Station: Coatdyke (10 minutes walk)
Nearest Bus Station: Coatbridge
Club Shop: At the ground
Opening Times: Wednesday 12.30pm to 3.30pm, Thursday 9.30am to 3.30pm and 9.30am to 12.30pm.
Telephone Nº: (01236) 606334

GROUND INFORMATION
Away Supporters' Entrances & Sections:
Main Street entrance for Main Stand accommodation

ADMISSION INFO (2024/2025 PRICES)
Adult Standing: £11.00
Adult Seating: £11.00
Student/Senior Citizen Standing/Seating: £6.00
Under-14s Standing/Seating: £3.00

DISABLED INFORMATION
Wheelchairs: Approximately 30 spaces available in the Disabled Area
Helpers: Admitted
Prices: Concessionary prices for the disabled. Helpers free
Disabled Toilets: Available at the East End of the Ground
Contact: (01236) 606334 (Bookings are advisable)

Travelling Supporters' Information:
Routes: From the East or West: Take the A8/M8 to the Shawhead Interchange then follow the A725 to the Town Centre. Follow A89 signs towards Airdrie at the roundabout, the ground is then on the left; From the South: Take the A725 from Bellshill/Hamilton/Motherwell/M74 to Coatbridge. Follow the A89 signs towards Airdrie at the roundabout, the ground is then on the left; From the North: Take the A73 to Airdrie then follow signs for the A8010 to Coatbridge. Join the A89 and the ground is one mile on the right.

BERWICK RANGERS FC

Founded: 1881
Nickname: 'The Borderers'
Ground: Shielfield Park, Shielfield Terrace, Tweedmouth, Berwick-upon-Tweed TD15 2EF
Ground Capacity: 4,099
Seating Capacity: 1,366
Record Attendance: 13,365 (28th January 1967)

Colours: Black and Gold Striped shirts, Black shorts
Matchday Telephone Nº: (01289) 307424 (12.00pm until 5.00pm)
Ticket Office: (01289) 307424
Website: berwickrangers.com
E-mail: club@berwickrangers.com

GENERAL INFORMATION
Car Parking: Large Car Park at the ground (free parking)
Coach Parking: At the ground
Nearest Railway Station: Berwick-upon-Tweed (1½ miles)
Nearest Bus Station: Berwick Town Centre (1 mile)
Club Shop: Inside the Stadium
Opening Times: Matchdays only from 2.00pm onwards (plus online sales)
Telephone Nº: (01289) 307424

GROUND INFORMATION
Away Supporters' Entrances & Sections:
Shielfield Terrace entrance for the Popular Side Terrace (Gates A or B), Gate B for Main Stand accommodation. Gate A is only used for selected matches.

ADMISSION INFO (2024/2025 PRICES)
Adult Standing: £10.00
Adult Seating: £10.00
Concessionary Seating/Standing: £5.00
Under-16s: Admitted free of charge

DISABLED INFORMATION
Wheelchairs: Spaces for 10 wheelchairs available in the disabled section
Helpers: Admitted
Prices: Concessionary prices are charge for disabled fans with helpers admitted free of charge
Disabled Toilets: Available between the turnstiles and the Grandstand entrance and behind the covered terracing. Also available in the Black & Gold Pub by the car park
Contact: (01289) 307424 (Bookings are appreciated) – Graham Exley (Disability Officer) – 07921 889052

Travelling Supporters' Information:
Routes: From the North: Take the A1 (Berwick Bypass), cross the new road-bridge then take the 1st exit at the roundabout. Carry on for approximately ¼ mile to the next roundabout, go straight across then continue for approximately ¼ mile into Shielfield Terrace. Turn left and the ground is on the left; From the South: Take the A1 Bypass and continue across the first roundabout signposted Scremerston/Tweedmouth and then on for 1 mile. At the crossroads/junction take B6354 'Spittal' Road right and continue for approx. 1 mile until the road becomes Shielfield Terrace. The ground is on the left in Shielfield Terrace.

BO'NESS UNITED FC

Founded: 1945
Nickname: 'The BU' (Bee-Yoo)
Ground: Newtown Park, 104 Jamieson Avenue, Bo'ness   EH51 0JX
Ground Capacity: 2,500   (No seating at present)
Record Attendance: 9,000 (vs Celtic on 5th March 1927 as Bo'ness FC)

Colours: Blue shirts with White shorts
Telephone Nº: 07545 347557
Website: www.bonessunitedfc.co.uk
E-mail: chrisveitchbufc@gmail.com

GENERAL INFORMATION
Car Parking: Street parking only
Coach Parking: Street parking only
Nearest Railway Station: Linlithgow (3 miles)
Nearest Bus Station: Bo'ness
Club Shop: RJM Sports, Unit 2b, West Mains Industrial Estate, Grangemouth   FK38 8TE
Opening Times: Weekdays 9.00am to 5.00pm (until 7.00pm on Thursdays)
Telephone Nº: (01324) 873804

GROUND INFORMATION
Away Supporters' Entrances & Sections:
No usual segregation

ADMISSION INFO (2024/2025 PRICES)
Adult Standing/Seating: £10.00
Concessionary Seating/Standing: £5.00
Note: Under-16s are admitted free of charge when accompanying a paying adult

DISABLED INFORMATION
Wheelchairs: Spaces available next to the Linlithgow Road entrance
Helpers: Admitted
Prices: Free of charge for both disabled fans and helpers
Disabled Toilets: Available next to the Linlithgow Road entrance
Contact: Chris Veitch – 07545 347557

Travelling Supporters' Information:
Routes: From the West: Take the A904 to Bo'ness and, upon reaching the outskirts of the town, turn right onto the A993 (Snab Brae) and continue as the road becomes Dean Road. After approximately ½ mile, turn right at the traffic lights onto the A706, heading towards Linlithgow. The first right after this is Jamieson Avenue and the ground is clearly visible on the right.

BROOMHILL FC

Founded: 2014
Former name BSC Glasgow
Nickname: 'The Baguettes'
Ground: Dumbarton Football Stadium, Castle Road, Dumbarton G82 1JJ
Ground Capacity: 2,020 (All Seats)

Colours: Yellow shirts and shorts
Telephone Nº: 07446 281332
Contact Address: G. Fraser, 44 Dykebar Avenue, Glasgow G13 3HF
Website: www.broomhillfc.com
E-mail: donald@broomhillfc.com

GENERAL INFORMATION
Car Parking: 400 spaces available at the ground (parking fee payable)
Coach Parking: At the ground
Nearest Railway Station: Dumbarton East
Nearest Bus Station: Dumbarton
Club Shop: None

GROUND INFORMATION
Away Supporters' Entrances & Sections: West Sections 1 and 2

ADMISSION INFO (2024/2025 PRICES)
Adult Standing/Seating: £10.00
Concessionary Standing/Seating: £5.00
Under-16s Standing/Seating: Free of charge
Note: Under-12s must be accompanied by an adult

DISABLED INFORMATION
Wheelchairs: Accommodated – 24 spaces available
Helpers: One admitted per disabled supporter
Prices: Free of charge disabled fans. Half-price for helpers
Disabled Toilets: Available
Contact: (01389) 762569

Travelling Supporters' Information:
Routes: The ground is situated just by Dumbarton Castle. Take the A814 into Dumbarton and follow the brown signs for the Castle to find the ground.

BROXBURN ATHLETIC FC

Unfortunately, no photograph of Albyn Park was available at the time of going to press.

Founded: 1894 (re-founded 1947)
Nickname: 'The Brox' or 'The Badgers'
Ground: Albyn Park, Greendykes Road, Broxburn, EH52 5BP
Ground Capacity: 2,050
Seating Capacity: none
Record Attendance: 1,400

Colours: Red shirts and White shorts
Telephone Nº: (01506) 858057
Mobile Contact Nº: 07753 708841
Website: www.broxburnathletic.co.uk
E-mail: info@broxburnathletic.co.uk

GENERAL INFORMATION
Car Parking: At the ground
Coach Parking: At the ground
Nearest Railway Station: Uphall (2 miles)
Club Shop: None

GROUND INFORMATION
Away Supporters' Entrances & Sections: No usual segregation

ADMISSION INFO (2024/2025 PRICES)
Adults: £10.00
Concessions: £6.00
Under-16s: Free (but must possess a season pass)

DISABLED INFORMATION
Wheelchairs: 4 covered spaces available within the stand
Helpers: Admitted
Prices: Concessionary prices for the disabled. Free for helpers
Disabled Toilets: Available
Contact: (01506) 858057 (Bookings are not necessary)

Travelling Supporters' Information:
Routes: From all directions: Exit the M9 at the Newbridge Interchange and take the A89 (Edinburgh Road) through Newbridge to Broxburn. At the roundabout take the 2nd exit along the A899 (Main Street) and continue to the junction with the B8020 (Greendykes Road) before turning right. Albyn Park is a short way along on the right close to the Union Canal.

CALEDONIAN BRAVES FC

Photo courtesy of Alastair Ross – Novantae Photography

Founded: 2011
Former Names: Edusport Academy
Nickname: None
Ground: Alliance Park, Strathclyde Country Park, Motherwell   ML1 3RB
Ground Capacity: 500
Seating Capacity: 100

Colours: Blue Shirts and shorts
Contact Number: 07843785312
Website: www.caledonianbraves.com
E-mail: info@caledonianbraves.com

GENERAL INFORMATION
Car Parking: Available at the ground
Coach Parking: Available at the ground
Nearest Railway Station: Bellshill (2 miles)
Nearest Bus Station: Motherwell
Club Shop: None

GROUND INFORMATION
Away Supporters' Entrances & Sections:
No usual segregation

ADMISSION INFO (2024/2025 PRICES)
Adult Standing: £5.00
Adult Seating: £5.00
Under-16s Standing/Seating: Free of charge
Concessionary Standing: £3.00
Concessionary Seating: £3.00

DISABLED INFORMATION
Wheelchairs: Accommodated
Helpers: Admitted
Prices: Concessionary prices are charged for disabled fans
Disabled Toilets: Available
Contact: 07843785312 (Bookings are necessary)

Travelling Supporters' Information:
Routes: Alliance Park is located at Bothwellhaugh Football Pitches in Strathclyde Country Park, just by Junction 5 of the M74. From All Directions: Exit the M74 at Junction 5 and follow the Brown Tourist Signs for Strathclyde Country Park. Follow the road, passing the Toby Carvery then take the first turning on the right, signposted Alliance Park and Bothwellhaugh.

CELTIC B FC

Ground: The Excelsior Stadium, Craigneuk Avenue, Airdrie ML6 8QZ
Ground Capacity: 9,843 (All seats)
Colours: Green & White hooped shirts, White shorts
Ticket Enquiries: (01236) 622000
Website: www.celticfc.com/celtic-b-team
E-mail: eoneill@celticfc.co.uk

GENERAL INFORMATION
Car Parking: Behind all the Stands
Coach Parking: Behind the East Stand
Nearest Railway Station: Drumgelloch (½ mile)
Nearest Bus Station: Gartlea – Airdrie Town Centre
Club Shop: At the ground
Opening Times: Opens at 12.00pm on Home Matchdays and Sunday 2.00pm – 4.00pm
Telephone Nº: (01236) 622000

GROUND INFORMATION
Away Supporters' Entrances & Sections:
The Jack Dalziel Stand and the Osprey Global East Stand

ADMISSION INFO (2024/2025 PRICES)
Adult Seating: £10.00
Under-16s Seating: £5.00
Senior Citizen/Concessionary Seating: £5.00

DISABLED INFORMATION
Wheelchairs: Spaces available for home and away fans accommodated in the front sections
Helpers: One admitted per disabled supporter
Prices: Concessionary prices for disabled fans with helpers admitted free of charge.
Disabled Toilets: Available in all the stands
Contact: (01236) 622000   (Bookings are preferable)

Travelling Supporters' Information:
Routes: From the East: Exit the M8 at Junction 6 and take the A73 (signposted for Cumbernauld). Pass through Chapelhall into Airdrie and turn right into Petersburn Road – the ground is on the left; From the West: Take the A8 to the Chapelhall turn-off for Chapelhall. Join the A73 at Chapelhall, then as above.

CIVIL SERVICE STROLLERS FC

Founded: 1908
Nickname: 'Strollers'
Ground: Christie Gillies Park, 25 Marine Drive, Edinburgh   EH4 5EJ
Ground Capacity: 1,596
Seating Capacity: 100

Colours: Red shirts and shorts
Contact Address: Keith Stewart, 117 Wester Broom Drive, Edinburgh   EH12 7RQ
Contact Phone N°: 07802 916832
Website: www.csstrollers.com
E-mail: keith.l.stewart@bt.com

GENERAL INFORMATION
Car Parking: At the ground
Coach Parking: At the ground
Nearest Railway Station: Edinburgh Waverley
Nearest Bus Station: St. Andrew's Square
Club Shop: E-mail tbpromotions1908@gmail.com

ADMISSION INFO (2024/2025 PRICES)
Adult Standing/Seating: £8.00
Concessionary Standing/Seating: £5.00
DISABLED INFORMATION
Wheelchairs: Accommodated
Helpers: Admitted
Prices: Concessionary prices are charged for both disabled fans and helpers
Disabled Toilets: Available
Contact: 07802 916832   (Bookings are not necessary)

Travelling Supporters' Information:
Routes: From the West: Take the A90 Queensferry Road into Edinburgh and continue until reaching the B9085 (Quality Street). Turn left into Quality Street and continue into Cramond Road. After ¼ mile turn right into Lauriston Farm Road. Continue to the roundabout and go left along Silver Knowes Road then into Marine Drive for the Ground; From the East: Take the A1 into Edinburgh and at the 1st roundabout take the 2nd exit into Milton Link. At the next roundabout (¼ mile) take 2nd exit onto A199 Sir Harry Lauder Road. Continue along A199 for approximately 2½ miles past Leith then join the A901 (Lindsay Road). Continue along A901 to the end of Lower Granton Road then take the 3rd exit at the roundabout into West Granton Road and after 1¼ mile take the 3rd exit at the roundabout into Marine Drive.

COWDENBEATH FC

Founded: 1880 (**Entered League**: 1905)
Nickname: 'Cowden' 'Blue Brazil" 'The Miners'
Ground: Central Park, High Street, Cowdenbeath KY4 9QQ
Ground Capacity: 4,370 **Seating Capacity**: 1,622
Record Attendance: 25,868 (21st September 1949)

Colours: Shirts are Royal Blue with White trim, Shorts are White
Telephone Nº: (01383) 610166
Ticket Office: (01383) 610166
Website: www.cowdenbeathfc.com
E-mail: office@cowdenbeathfc.com

GENERAL INFORMATION
Car Parking: 93 spaces available at the ground and Stenhouse Street (200 yards) has 190 spaces available.
Coach Parking: King Street and Rowan Terrace
Nearest Railway Station: Cowdenbeath (400 yards)
Nearest Bus Station: Cowdenbeath (Bus Stop at ground)
Club Shop: At the ground and also at Beath Bargain Store, High Street, Cowdenbath
Opening Times: Matchdays only (at the ground)
Telephone Nº: (01383) 610166

GROUND INFORMATION
Away Supporters' Entrances & Sections:
High Street end of the ground

ADMISSION INFO (2024/2025 PRICES)
Adult Standing/Seating: £12.00
Child Standing/Seating: £7.00 (Ages 16 and under)
Senior Citizen Standing/Seating: £7.00
Note: Advance prices are £1.00 less.

DISABLED INFORMATION
Wheelchairs: Accommodated in the North Stand
Helpers: Admitted
Prices: Concessionary prices are charged for disabled fans. Helpers are admitted free of charge
Disabled Toilets: Available
Contact: (01383) 610166 (Bookings are necessary) –
John Cameron (Disability Officer): office@cowdenbeathfc.com

Travelling Supporters' Information:
Routes: Exit the M90 at Junction 3 for Dunfermline. Take the Dual Carriageway to Cowdenbeath and follow straight on into the High Street. The ground is situated on the first left turn in the High Street.

CUMBERNAULD COLTS FC

Founded: 1969 (**Entered League**: 2015)
Nickname: 'Colts'
Ground: Broadwood Stadium, Ardgoil Drive, Cumbernauld, Glasgow   G68 9NE
Ground Capacity: 8,086 (all seats)
Record Attendance: 8,000 (14th August 1996)

Colours: Yellow Shirts with Blue shorts
Contact Address: Stewart McKenzie,
8 Lime Crescent, Cumbernauld   G67 3PQ
Telephone N°: (01236) 451511 or 07798 646110
Website: www.cumbernauldcoltsfc.com
E-mail: admin@cumbernauld-colts.com

GENERAL INFORMATION
Car Parking: Behind the Main and West Stands
Coach Parking: Behind the Main Stand
Nearest Railway Station: Croy (1½ miles)
Nearest Bus Station: Cumbernauld Town Centre
Club Shop: Online via website

GROUND INFORMATION
Away Supporters' Entrances & Sections:
No usual segregation

ADMISSION INFO (2024/2025 PRICES)
Adult Seating: £10.00
Concessionary Seating: £5.00
Note: Under-16s are admitted free with a paying adult

DISABLED INFORMATION
Wheelchairs: 10 spaces each for home and away fans accommodated in front sections of each stand
Helpers: One helper admitted per wheelchair
Prices: Concessionary prices apply for disabled fans. Helpers are admitted free of charge
Disabled Toilets: 4 available in the Main and West Stands
Contact: 07798 646110   (Bookings are not necessary)

Travelling Supporters' Information:
Routes: From all Parts: Exit the A80 at Broadwood Junction and follow the signs for Broadwood. The ground is signposted from the next roundabout.

EAST KILBRIDE FC

Founded: 2010
Nickname: 'The Kilby' or 'EK'
Ground: K Park Training Academy, Calderglen Country Park, East Kilbride   G75 0QZ
Telephone N°: (01355) 279204
Ground Capacity: 660
Seating Capacity: 400
Record Attendance: 330 (2013/2014 season)

Colours: Blue and Gold halved shirts, Blue shorts
Contact Address: Dave McKenna, 21 Kirkton Gate, East Kilbride   G74 1NF
Contact Mobile N°: 07800 948932
Website: www.eastkilbridefootballclub.co.uk
E-mail: ekfc@outlook.com

GENERAL INFORMATION
Car Parking: At the ground
Coach Parking: At the ground
Nearest Railway Station: East Kilbride (2 miles)
Nearest Bus Station: East Kilbride (2 miles)
Club Shop: At the ground
Opening Times:: Matchdays only (plus online sales via the website)

GROUND INFORMATION
Away Supporters' Entrances & Sections:
No usual segregation

ADMISSION INFO (2024/2025 PRICES)
Adult Standing: £8.00
Adult Seating: £8.00
Concessionary Standing: £4.00
Concessionary Seating: £4.00

DISABLED INFORMATION
Wheelchairs: Accommodated
Helpers: Admitted
Prices: Normal prices apply for disabled fans. Helpers are admitted free of charge
Disabled Toilets: Available
Contact: 07757859368 Peter Hickey (Bookings are not necessary)

Travelling Supporters' Information:
Routes: From the East: Take the A726 into East Kilbride after passing the East Kilbride Shopping Centre, continue straight on at the first roundabout then take the 2nd exit at the next roundabout onto Strathaven Road (still the A726). After a short distance, turn left into Calderglen Country Park at the brown tourist sign. From the South: Take the A726 northwards from Strathaven. Upon entering the outskirts of East Kilbride, turn right into Calderglen Country Park at the brown tourist sign. From the North and East: Take the A749/A725 to East Kilbride and follow the A725 towards the south of the town. Turn left onto the A726 signposted for Strathaven and follow a short distance before turning left into Calderglen Country Park.

EAST STIRLINGSHIRE FC

East Stirlingshire are groundsharing with Falkirk for the 2024/2025 season.

Founded: 1880
Former Names: Bainsford Britannia FC
Nickname: 'The Shire'
Ground: The Falkirk Stadium, 4 Stadium Way, Falkirk FK2 9EE
Ground Capacity: 7,937 (All seats)
Record Attendance: 12,000 (21/2/1921 – Firs Park)

Colours: Black and White hooped shirts, Black shorts
Postal Address: c/o The Falkirk Stadium, 4 Stadium Way, Falkirk, FK2 9EE
Telephone Nº: 07985197766
Website: www.es-fc.co.uk
E-mail: commercial@es-fc.co.uk

GENERAL INFORMATION
Car Parking: A large Car Park is adjacent
Coach Parking: Available at the rear of the North Stand
Nearest Railway Station: Falkirk Grahamston (1 mile)
Nearest Bus Station: Falkirk (1 mile)
Club Shop: At the office (see above for details)
Opening Times: Weekdays from 9.00am to 3.00pm
Telephone Nº: (01324) 871171

GROUND INFORMATION
Away Supporters' Entrances & Sections: No usual segregation

ADMISSION INFO (2024/2025 PRICES)
Adult Standing: £10.00
Adult Seating: £10.00
Concessionary Standing: £7.00
Concessionary Seating: £7.00
Under-14s Standing/Seating: Free with a paying adult

DISABLED INFORMATION
Wheelchairs: Accommodated
Helpers: One helper admitted for each disabled fan
Prices: Concessionary prices for the disabled. Free for helpers
Disabled Toilets: Available in the Main Stand
Contact: 07985197766 (Bookings are necessary)

Travelling Supporters' Information:
Routes: Exit the M9 at Junction 6 and take the A904 towards Falkirk. Continue into Falkirk at the Westfield/Laurieston roundabout along Grangemouth Road and take the first right into Alexander Avenue. Then take the 2nd right into Westfield Street and the ground is on the right.

GALA FAIRYDEAN ROVERS FC

Founded: 1907
Nickname: 'The Braw Lads' 'The Fairies'
Ground: The 3G Arena, Nether Road, Netherdale, Galashiels TD1 3HE
Ground Capacity: 2,000
Seating Capacity: 460
Record Attendance: 6,000 (vs Rangers in 1989)

Colours: Red and Black shirts with White shorts
Ground Telephone N°: None
Contact: Robert Fairburn (Match Secretary)
Contact Phone N°: 07767 645354
Website: www.gfrfc.co.uk
E-mail: matchsecretary@gfrfc.co.uk

GENERAL INFORMATION
Car Parking: Available at the ground
Coach Parking: Available at the ground
Nearest Railway Station: Galashiels (1½ miles)
Nearest Bus Station: Galashiels
Club Shop: None - online only.

GROUND INFORMATION
Away Supporters' Entrances & Sections:
No usual segregation

ADMISSION INFO (2024/2025 PRICES)
Adult Standing/Seating: £10.00
Concessionary Standing/Seating: £5.00
Note: Under-16s are admitted free of charge when accompanying a paying adult

DISABLED INFORMATION
Wheelchairs: Accommodated with entrance via the North turnstile
Helpers: Admitted
Prices: Normal prices apply for disabled fans. Helpers free
Disabled Toilets: Available in the Main Stand
Contact: 07767 645354 – Robert Fairburn
(Bookings are not necessary)

Travelling Supporters' Information:
Routes: From Edinburgh: Take the A7 to Galashiels and follow signs for Heriot-Watt University and Netherdale. After passing the Fire Station on the left, turn-off left at the mini-roundabout along Tweed Road and the ground is ½ mile on the left; From Jedburgh/Hawick: Take the A7 to Galashiels and turn right at the mini-roundabout for the ground.

GRETNA FC 2008

Founded: 2007
Nickname: 'Black and Whites'
Ground: Raydale Park, Gretna Community Sports Hub, Dominion Road, Gretna DG16 5AP
Ground Capacity: 1,030
Seating Capacity: 138

Record Attendance: 653 (2009)
Colours: Black and White Hooped shirts, Black shorts
Contact Mobile Nº: 07902 826124
Website: www.gretnafc2008.co.uk
E-mail: kevinsmith@gretnafc2008.co.uk

GENERAL INFORMATION
Car Parking: At the ground
Coach Parking: At the ground
Nearest Railway Station: Gretna Green (1 mile)
Nearest Bus Station: Carlisle (10 miles)
Club Shop: At the ground
Opening Times: Matchdays only
Telephone Nº: –

GROUND INFORMATION
Away Supporters' Entrances & Sections:
West Enclosure

ADMISSION INFO (2024/2025 PRICES)
Adult Standing/Seating: £8.00
Concessions Standing/Seating: £6.00
Under-16s Standing/Seating: Free of charge

DISABLED INFORMATION
Wheelchairs: Accommodated
Helpers: Admitted
Prices: Normal prices apply for disabled fans.
Disabled Toilets: Available
Contact: 07973 105818

Travelling Supporters' Information:
Routes: From All Parts: Leave the A74 at the Gretna turn-off and exit onto the B7076. Cross Border Bridge with the Gretna Chase Hotel on the right then turn left at the Gretna Inn into Annan Road. After ¼ mile turn left into Dominion Road and the ground is on the right.

HEART OF MIDLOTHIAN B FC

Ground: Ainslie Park, 94 Pilton Drive, Edinburgh, EH5 2HF
Ground Phone N°: 0131 552 7854
Ground Capacity: 3,500
Seating Capacity: 534

Colours: Shirts are Maroon, White shorts
Contact Phone N°: 07792 917108
Website: www.heartsfc.co.uk
E-mail: shelleykay@homplc.co.uk

GENERAL INFORMATION
Car Parking: At the ground
Coach Parking: At the ground by prior arrangement
Nearest Railway Station: Edinburgh Waverley (2.75 miles)
Nearest Bus Station: St. Andrew's Square, Edinburgh
Club Shop: Website sales only

GROUND INFORMATION
Away Supporters' Entrances & Sections:
No usual segregation

ADMISSION INFO (2024/2025 PRICES)
Adult Standing/Seating: £5.00
Concessionary Standing/Seating: £2.00
Child Standing/Seating: Free

DISABLED INFORMATION
Wheelchairs: Accommodated
Helpers: Please phone the club for details
Prices: Please phone the club for details
Disabled Toilets: Available
Contact: 07719 032111   (Bookings are not necessary)

Travelling Supporters' Information:
Routes: From Edinburgh: Take the A6094 into Rosewell. In Rosewell, turn left then left again opposite St. Matthews Roman Catholic Primary School. The ground is situated next to Ferguson Park Garage.

LINLITHGOW ROSE FC

Founded: 1889
Nicknames: The Rose, Rosey Posey & The Gallant
Ground: MV Commercial Prestonfield Stadium, Braehead Road, Linlithgow   EH49 6HF
Ground Capacity: 2,264
Seating Capacity: 301

Record Attendance: 3,526 vs Petershill
Colours: Maroon shirts with White shorts
Telephone Nº: 01506 0843736 (Social Club)
Website: www.linlithgowrose.co.uk
E-mail: lrfc1889secretary@gmail.com

GENERAL INFORMATION
Car Parking: Space at the ground is limited but Linlithgow Academy which is close by has extensive car parking available.
Coach Parking: At the ground
Nearest Railway Station: Linlithgow (1 mile)
Buses: Service 38 Edinburgh to Stirling stops at West Port which is a 5 minute walk away.
Club Shop: Online only

GROUND INFORMATION
Away Supporters' Entrances & Sections:
No usual segregation

ADMISSION INFO (2024/2025 PRICES)
Adult Standing: £10.00
Adult Seating: £11.50
Concessionary Standing: £7.00
Concessionary Seating: £8.00
Unaccompanied Children aged 12 to 16: £7.00
Note: Under-16s are admitted free with a paying Adult and all Under-12s must be accompanied.

DISABLED INFORMATION
Wheelchairs: Accommodated – 6 wheelchair spaces
Helpers: Admitted
Prices: Free of charge for disabled fans. Half-price for helpers
Disabled Toilets: 2 available
Contact: via e-mail   (Bookings are not necessary)

Travelling Supporters' Information:
Routes: From the East: Exit the M9 at Junction 3 taking the A803 into Linlithgow. Pass the Railway Station on the left and continue along High Street until reaching the West Port Hotel, then turn left along Preston Road before taking a right turn into Braehead Road for the ground; From the West: Exit M9 at Junction 4 taking the A803 to Linlithgow. Continue along, passing Sainsburys and St.Ninians Church on the left before reaching the West Port Hotel then turn right into Preston Road and continue as from the East.

TRANENT FC

Founded: 1911
Nickname: The Belters
Former name: Tranent Juniors FC
Ground: Foresters Park, 72A Lindores Drive, Tranent   EH33 1JB
Ground Capacity: 2,300   **Seating Capacity**: 44

Record Attendance: 5,300 vs Cumnock
Colours: Maroon shirts and shorts
Contact No: 07591 916199
Website: www.tranentjuniorsfc.co.uk
E-mail: drummondgraham0@gmail.com

GENERAL INFORMATION
Car Parking: At the ground and the nearby Loch Centre
Coach Parking: At the ground
Nearest Railway Station: Wallyford
Buses: Lothian buses serve Tranent and stop in the High Street.

GROUND INFORMATION
Away Supporters' Entrances & Sections: No usual segregation

ADMISSION INFO (2024/2025 PRICES)
Adult Standing: £10.00   **Adult Seating**: £10.00
Concessionary Standing: £7.00
Concessionary Seating: £7.00

DISABLED INFORMATION
Wheelchairs: Accommodated
Helpers: Admitted
Prices: Free of charge for disabled fans. Half-price for helpers
Disabled Toilets: 2 available
Contact: (Bookings are not necessary)

Travelling Supporters' Information:
Routes: Exit the Meadowhill turn-off and follow the A198 South into Tranent passing the Fire Station on the right. Continue along Church Street then turn left after passing the Town Hall along Winton Place. Pass the Library on the left then take the 2nd left into Lindores Drive and the ground is on the left.

UNIVERSITY OF STIRLING FC

Founded: 2008
Nickname: None
Ground: Forthbank Stadium, Springkerse, Stirling, FK7 7UJ
Ground Capacity: 3,808
Seating Capacity: 2,508
Record Attendance: 3,808 (17th February 1996)

Colours: Green shirts and shorts
Contact Address: Chris Geddes, Gannochy Sports Centre, University of Stirling, Stirling FK9 4LA
Contact Phone N°: (01786) 466511 or 0773 904-9047
Website: www.stirlingunifc.stir.ac.uk
E-mail: chris.geddes@stir.ac.uk

GENERAL INFORMATION
Car Parking: At the ground and Springkerse Retail Park (5 to 10 minutes walk)
Coach Parking: Adjacent to the ground
Nearest Railway Station: Stirling (2 miles)
Nearest Bus Station: Stirling (2 miles)
Club Shop: None

GROUND INFORMATION
Away Supporters' Entrances & Sections: South Terracing and East Stand

ADMISSION INFO (2024/2025 PRICES)
Adult Seating: £8.00
Child Seating: £5.00
Concessionary Seating: £5.00

DISABLED INFORMATION
Wheelchairs: Accommodated
Helpers: Admitted
Prices: Concessionary prices are charged for disabled fans. Helpers are admitted free of charge
Disabled Toilets: Available
Contact: 0773 904-9047 (Bookings are not necessary)

Travelling Supporters' Information:
Routes: Follow signs for Stirling from the M9/M80 Northbound. From Pirnhall Roundabout follow signs for Alloa/St. Andrew's to the 4th roundabout and then turn left for the stadium.

Scottish Premiership 2023-2024 season

	Aberdeen	Celtic	Dundee	Heart of Midlothian	Hibernian	Kilmarnock	Livingston	Motherwell	Rangers	Ross County	St. Johnstone	St. Mirren
Aberdeen	■	1-3	1-1	2-1	0-2	0-1	2-1	3-3	1-1	4-0	0-0	0-3
	■	1-1	0-0		2-2		5-1	1-0		2-1	0-2	
	■										1-0	
Celtic	6-0	■	3-0	0-2	4-1	3-1	2-0	1-1	2-1	4-2	0-0	2-1
		■	7-1	3-0		1-1			2-1	1-0	3-1	3-0
		■										3-2
Dundee	1-0	0-3	■	1-0	1-2	2-2	1-0	1-1	0-5	0-0	2-1	4-0
		1-2	■	2-3		2-2		2-3	0-0	2-0		1-3
			■		1-1							
Heart of Midlothian	2-0	1-4	3-2	■	2-2	0-0	1-0	0-1	0-1	2-2	1-0	2-0
	2-0	2-0	3-0	■	1-1	1-1	4-2	2-0	3-3			
Hibernian	2-0	0-0	0-0	0-1	■	1-0	2-3	2-2	0-3	2-2	2-0	2-3
	0-4	1-2	2-1		■		3-0	3-0		2-0	1-2	0-3
Kilmarnock	2-0	2-1	2-2	0-1	2-2	■	3-1	1-0	1-0	0-1	2-1	1-1
	2-0	0-5		0-0	2-2	■		1-0		1-2	1-0	5-2
Livingston	0-0	0-3	0-2	1-2	0-1	0-0	■	2-0	0-2	2-2	0-0	1-1
	0-0	0-3	1-4		1-1		■	1-3		2-0	2-1	1-0
Motherwell	2-4	1-2	3-3	1-2	2-1	2-1	3-1	■	0-2	3-3	1-1	0-1
	0-1	1-3			1-1	1-1	4-1	■		5-0	1-2	1-1
Rangers	1-3	0-1	3-1	2-1	4-0	3-1	4-0	1-0	■	3-1	2-0	2-0
	2-1	3-3	5-2	5-0	3-1	4-1	3-0	1-2	■			
Ross County	0-3	0-3	0-1	0-1	2-2	0-0	1-1	3-0	0-2	■	2-0	1-0
	2-2			2-1	2-1		3-2	1-5	3-2	■	0-1	1-1
St. Johnstone	1-1	1-3	2-2	0-2	1-0	2-1	1-1	2-2	0-2	1-0	■	1-0
			1-2	0-1	1-3	0-2	1-1	1-1	0-3	1-1	■	
St. Mirren	2-2	0-3	2-1	1-0	2-2	0-1	1-0	0-0	0-3	2-0	4-0	■
	2-1		2-0	1-2		0-1		0-1		2-0		■
				2-2			1-2					■

Scottish Premiership

Season 2023/2024

Team	P	W	D	L	F	A	Pts
CELTIC	38	29	6	3	95	30	93
Rangers	38	27	4	7	87	32	85
Heart of Midlothian	38	20	8	10	54	42	68
Kilmarnock	38	14	14	10	46	44	56
St. Mirren	38	13	8	17	46	52	47
Dundee	38	10	12	16	49	68	42
Aberdeen	38	12	12	14	48	52	48
Hibernian	38	11	13	14	52	59	46
Motherwell	38	10	13	15	56	59	43
St. Johnstone	38	8	11	19	29	54	35
Ross County	38	8	11	19	38	67	35
Livingston	**38**	**5**	**10**	**23**	**29**	**70**	**25**

With 5 games of the season left, the Premiership was split into two groups of 6.
The top half contended for the title while the bottom half decided relegation.

Scottish Championship 2023-2024 season	Airdrieonians	Arbroath	Ayr United	Dundee United	Dunfermline Athletic	Greenock Morton	Inverness Caledonian Thistle	Partick Thistle	Queens Park	Raith Rovers
Airdrieonians		2-0	1-2	0-2	1-2	0-0	2-1	2-1	1-1	1-0
		5-2	2-3	0-0	2-1	3-1	2-0	1-1	1-1	1-0
Arbroath	4-0		2-1	0-4	1-1	1-2	2-3	1-3	0-1	1-2
	1-2		0-0	0-3	2-3	1-2	1-1	0-1	0-5	3-2
Ayr United	1-0	2-0		0-3	2-2	0-1	1-0	0-4	2-2	1-2
	2-1	5-0		1-2	3-3	1-1	1-3	4-3	1-2	1-2
Dundee United	2-0	6-0	1-0		1-1	1-1	1-1	3-0	4-1	0-1
	0-2	4-0	1-0		0-0	2-3	1-1	4-1	3-1	2-0
Dunfermline Athletic	2-1	3-0	0-1	1-2		3-1	1-1	1-2	0-3	0-1
	0-2	1-1	2-0	3-1		0-5	1-1	1-1	0-0	1-2
Greenock Morton	0-1	0-3	3-1	0-1	1-2		2-1	1-4	1-0	1-2
	2-1	3-0	3-0	1-4	0-1		0-2	1-1	2-0	0-0
Inverness Caledonian Thistle	1-0	1-2	3-1	0-1	1-1	0-0		0-0	1-2	1-2
	0-0	2-1	1-2	0-1	0-0	3-1		3-3	0-1	0-1
Partick Thistle	2-1	0-3	2-2	0-5	3-0	2-1	1-1		3-1	2-2
	4-0	4-0	0-0	1-1	1-3	2-1	1-0		3-2	0-1
Queen's Park	1-2	2-1	2-5	0-0	0-2	0-0	1-4	2-2		2-3
	2-0	6-0	1-2	0-5	2-1	0-0	0-1	2-2		0-0
Raith Rovers	1-1	2-2	4-4	1-1	1-0	3-2	1-0	4-3	3-2	
	1-3	5-0	2-1	2-1	2-0	0-0	2-3	0-0	1-2	

Scottish Championship
Season 2023/2024

Dundee United		36	22	9	5	73	23	75
Raith Rovers		36	20	9	7	58	42	69
Partick Thistle		36	14	13	9	63	54	55
Airdrieonians		36	15	7	14	44	44	52
Greenock Morton		36	12	9	15	43	46	45
Dunfermline Athletic		36	11	12	13	43	48	45
Ayr United		36	12	8	16	53	61	44
Queen's Park		36	11	10	15	50	56	43
Inverness Caledonian Thistle		*36*	*10*	*12*	*14*	*41*	*40*	*42*
Arbroath		*36*	*6*	*5*	*25*	*35*	*89*	*23*

Scottish League One
2023-2024 Season

	Alloa Athletic	Annan Athletic	Cove Rangers	Edinburgh City	Falkirk	Hamilton Academical	Kelty Hearts	Montrose	Queen of the South	Stirling Albion
Alloa Athletic		2-1	1-0	1-1	1-4	0-0	3-1	2-2	1-0	0-1
		1-1	4-1	3-1	0-5	0-1	3-0	0-0	0-2	1-0
Annan Athletic	1-1		1-3	3-2	0-3	1-2	2-2	1-3	0-1	3-0
	2-3		4-2	3-0	3-3	1-3	3-2	2-2	2-1	2-1
Cove Rangers	1-2	3-2		7-2	2-2	1-0	2-2	1-0	1-2	3-1
	2-3	2-1		3-1	0-1	1-3	2-2	1-4	0-2	4-2
Edinburgh City	3-0	3-2	2-2		0-2	0-3	1-4	1-5	1-2	1-3
	2-5	1-2	0-2		2-2	2-5	0-3	1-0	1-1	1-3
Falkirk	3-0	3-0	4-0	2-1		0-0	2-1	3-2	1-0	3-0
	2-2	1-1	5-1	4-1		3-2	2-2	3-0	1-0	5-0
Hamilton Academical	2-1	5-0	1-0	1-1	1-3		1-1	1-0	5-0	5-0
	1-2	2-3	2-0	1-0	0-2		4-1	1-1	0-0	3-0
Kelty Hearts	2-1	1-1	0-1	3-2	1-5	0-2		0-1	3-1	1-0
	2-1	1-1	0-1	3-1	0-1	0-5		0-2	0-0	1-0
Montrose	2-1	1-1	0-3	5-2	0-0	0-3	0-2		1-4	1-0
	4-3	1-1	1-1	3-0	1-7	1-2	4-2		3-2	0-1
Queen of the South	3-4	3-1	0-1	3-1	1-1	1-2	1-3	2-3		0-1
	1-1	2-1	2-0	2-0	1-4	0-2	1-2	2-3		2-2
Stirling Albion	0-2	1-1	2-2	1-0	1-2	2-2	1-0	0-2	1-1	
	1-5	1-1	2-2	4-0	1-2	0-0	5-0	1-0	0-0	

Scottish League League One
Season 2023/2024

Falkirk	36	27	9	0	96	28	90
Hamilton Academical	36	22	8	6	73	28	74
Alloa Athletic	36	16	8	12	60	55	56
Montrose	36	15	8	13	58	57	53
Cove Rangers	36	14	7	15	58	63	49
Kelty Hearts	36	12	8	16	48	63	44
Queen of the South	36	11	8	17	46	53	41
Annan Athletic	36	9	12	15	55	68	39
Stirling Albion	*36*	*10*	*9*	*17*	*39*	*58*	*39*
Edinburgh City	*36*	*3*	*5*	*28*	*38*	*98*	*8*

Edinburgh City had 6 points deducted after failing to pay players on time, defaulting on tax obligations to HMRC and then failing to engage fully in the disciplinary process.

Scottish League Two
2023-2024 Season

	Bonnyrigg Rose	Clyde	Dumbarton	East Fife	Elgin City	Forfar Athletic	Peterhead	Stenhousemuir	Stranraer	The Spartans
Bonnyrigg Rose		3-2	1-1	4-2	5-1	0-2	1-1	0-1	1-1	2-2
		1-2	1-1	0-2	2-0	4-0	2-2	0-1	0-0	0-1
Clyde	0-2		0-4	0-3	2-1	0-0	1-2	1-2	2-2	1-2
	3-2		2-0	1-0	2-1	0-2	1-1	2-2	1-0	0-0
Dumbarton	4-0	4-4		1-0	1-0	3-1	0-1	0-1	3-1	1-1
	2-0	1-0		1-2	2-2	2-2	1-0	0-0	2-1	0-0
East Fife	0-3	2-0	0-1		4-0	1-1	0-3	0-2	4-0	0-3
	1-4	1-1	3-2		2-0	1-1	2-2	1-1	2-1	1-2
Elgin City	2-0	2-1	2-0	1-1		1-0	2-1	1-1	0-1	0-4
	1-0	0-3	0-1	1-0		1-1	1-1	2-2	2-1	2-2
Forfar Athletic	1-2	1-1	2-4	0-0	0-0		1-3	1-3	1-1	2-2
	0-0	2-1	0-2	2-1	2-1		3-3	1-1	2-0	1-0
Peterhead	2-1	2-1	3-1	2-0	6-0	1-2		0-0	3-2	0-1
	0-0	4-1	2-1	1-1	1-1	2-1		2-1	2-0	0-1
Stenhousemuir	1-0	2-2	2-4	2-1	2-0	0-0	2-0		5-0	3-2
	1-1	1-6	1-0	0-0	1-1	2-1	0-0		1-0	0-0
Stranraer	3-1	1-0	5-0	1-1	3-1	0-2	2-1	0-3		3-4
	1-1	2-0	0-0	0-1	1-2	0-0	2-0	2-0		1-2
The Spartans	2-2	1-1	2-0	2-2	2-1	1-0	1-2	0-1	3-0	
	2-1	1-1	2-6	1-3	1-2	1-0	2-2	0-2	0-0	

Scottish League League Two
Season 2023/2024

Stenhousemuir	36	18	14	4	50	31	68
Peterhead	36	16	12	8	58	39	60
The Spartans	36	15	13	8	53	43	58
Dumbarton	36	16	9	11	56	44	57
East Fife	36	11	11	14	46	47	44
Forfar Athletic	36	9	15	12	38	45	42
Elgin City	36	10	10	16	35	59	40
Bonnyrigg Rose	36	9	12	15	47	48	39
Clyde	36	9	11	16	46	58	38
Stranraer	36	9	9	18	38	53	36

Highland Football League 2023-2024 Season	Banks o'Dee	Brechin City	Brora Rangers	Buckie Thistle	Clachnacuddin	Deveronvale	Formartine United	Forres Mechanics	Fraserburgh	Huntly	Inverurie Loco Works	Keith	Lossiemouth	Nairn County	Rothes	Strathspey Thistle	Turriff United	Wick Academy
Banks o' Dee	■	0-1	2-2	2-0	2-2	4-1	2-1	4-0	2-0	2-1	3-0	2-0	1-1	3-0	4-0	4-1	3-2	4-0
Brechin City	0-0	■	2-1	2-3	6-0	5-1	1-0	6-1	0-1	5-0	2-1	3-1	2-0	2-0	3-1	5-0	5-1	3-1
Brora Rangers	1-2	1-2	■	1-5	1-0	3-3	1-4	3-2	1-2	3-0	1-1	4-1	3-2	2-1	1-0	3-1	4-2	1-0
Buckie Thistle	2-1	2-1	2-0	■	2-3	6-1	2-0	3-1	1-0	3-0	1-1	1-0	3-0	6-0	3-1	6-1	4-0	5-2
Clachnacuddin	1-0	0-2	0-2	2-3	■	2-2	0-5	1-4	2-6	2-4	2-4	3-1	2-0	0-1	0-1	4-4	1-5	8-0
Deveronvale	3-3	0-4	0-3	0-0	0-0	■	0-3	1-1	2-4	0-6	2-1	1-0	3-1	1-3	2-2	0-3	0-1	0-0
Formartine United	1-4	4-3	3-3	1-1	3-0	5-0	■	2-0	2-2	2-1	1-1	6-2	2-2	5-1	6-1	4-0	2-4	3-1
Forres Mechanics	2-2	1-1	0-1	1-8	1-1	0-2	0-4	■	1-2	2-2	0-1	2-1	1-1	0-0	0-1	2-1	1-0	3-1
Fraserburgh	2-1	4-2	2-0	1-3	2-2	3-2	1-2	2-1	■	6-0	4-2	3-0	3-1	3-0	5-0	11ñ0	3-0	3-0
Huntly	1-3	2-2	1-0	2-3	8-0	5-1	0-1	3-0	4-1	■	1-2	1-1	2-1	0-0	4-4	7-0	4-2	2-1
Inverurie Loco Works	0-2	0-2	2-2	0-2	1-0	3-0	1-2	1-0	0-7	2-3	■	1-2	1-1	6-0	0-1	5-0	1-4	3-1
Keith	1-3	0-1	0-1	0-3	1-1	3-2	2-3	1-1	2-2	1-0	1-2	■	1-0	1-1	2-1	3-1	1-0	0-4
Lossiemouth	1-6	0-3	1-1	2-1	5-3	3-3	1-2	0-3	0-1	1-3	0-1	1-0	■	1-4	3-1	2-1	0-0	1-0
Nairn County	3-3	0-1	0-1	3-0	1-1	4-2	0-2	2-1	0-3	2-4	4-0	3-2	5-1	■	0-2	4-1	2-1	2-0
Rothes	2-2	0-2	0-1	1-3	3-2	2-1	2-2	1-1	0-3	1-4	1-4	0-0	1-0	0-3	■	8-2	1-3	3-0
Strathspey Thistle	0-6	1-6	1-10	0-7	2-1	5-2	0-1	0-2	1-5	1-4	0-2	1-2	0-3	0-4	2-4	■	1-8	1-6
Turriff United	0-4	0-3	2-2	1-3	4-1	1-3	1-2	2-0	3-2	4-0	4-1	1-2	0-0	1-3	3-1	7-1	■	3-1
Wick Academy	1-1	1-2	0-0	3-1	3-0	2-2	3-1	3-2	0-3	2-2	2-1	2-0	3-0	2-3	0-0	3-2	1-5	■

Highland Football League
Season 2023/2024

Buckie Thistle	34	26	3	5	98	34	81
Brechin City	34	26	3	5	90	28	81
Fraserburgh	34	25	3	6	102	37	78
Banks o' Dee	34	21	9	4	87	33	72
Formartine United	34	22	6	6	87	43	72
Brora Rangers	34	17	8	9	64	46	59
Huntly	34	16	6	12	81	61	54
Nairn County	34	16	5	13	59	58	53
Turriff United	34	15	3	16	75	63	48
Inverurie Loco Works	34	13	5	16	52	58	44
Rothes	34	10	7	17	47	71	37
Wick Academy	34	10	6	18	49	70	36
Keith	34	9	6	19	35	61	33
Forres Mechanics	34	7	9	18	37	64	30
Lossiemouth	34	7	8	19	36	66	29
Deveronvale	34	5	10	19	43	91	25
Clachnacuddin	34	5	8	21	47	89	23
Strathspey Thistle	34	3	1	30	35	151	10

Lowland Football League 2023-2024 season	Albion Rovers	Berwick Rangers	Boíness United	Broomhill	Caledonian Braves	Celtic B	Civil Service Strollers	Cowdenbeath	Cumbernauld Colts	East Kilbride	East Stirlingshire	Edinburgh University	Gala Fairydean Rovers	Gretna 2008	Heart of Midlothian "B"	Linlithgow Rose	Tranent	University of Stirling
Albion Rovers		1-0	0-0	2-1	2-1	1-1	1-2	0-1	1-0	0-2	3-1	1-2	3-0	1-0	1-2	3-0	1-3	0-1
Berwick Rangers	2-1		1-2	4-0	0-2	2-1	1-0	0-2	0-0	0-1	1-2	2-0	3-3	3-0	2-2	1-2	2-2	2-2
Boíness United	0-1	5-1		3-0	2-1	1-0	3-2	4-2	0-3	3-4	4-2	3-1	3-0	2-0	3-3	0-0	0-2	3-2
Broomhill	1-1	2-0	1-1		2-0	1-2	4-2	0-1	2-2	1-6	3-1	4-0	2-3	4-1	1-2	2-0	1-3	0-4
Caledonian Braves	1-1	1-0	1-2	3-1		4-2	0-1	3-2	1-2	1-2	0-1	4-2	2-1	4-0	2-1	0-1	2-2	0-0
Celtic B	2-1	1-0	3-1	2-0	5-1		7-0	2-2	3-0	0-2	1-2	4-0	5-0	7-0	2-1	3-0	2-1	1-0
Civil Service Strollers	1-0	1-0	2-0	0-3	1-1	3-1		1-1	3-1	2-1	0-0	3-1	7-0	1-0	2-3	2-1	1-2	0-2
Cowdenbeath	0-0	1-4	0-2	0-0	2-2	3-3	2-2		0-2	2-1	1-2	7-1	2-2	2-1	2-1	1-1	0-2	2-2
Cumbernauld Colts	1-1	2-1	2-1	2-1	2-0	1-0	0-0	4-2		1-2	1-1	4-1	2-1	6-0	1-2	1-1	1-5	3-3
East Kilbride	1-3	1-0	0-2	2-1	0-0	2-1	2-0	4-2	2-0		2-1	7-4	4-2	4-1	2-4	2-1	3-2	4-2
East Stirlingshire	3-2	1-2	3-4	3-4	1-1	6-4	0-2	2-3	0-3	0-2		3-1	0-1	3-2	1-1	2-1	1-2	2-3
Edinburgh University	2-2	1-3	2-4	1-1	1-3	1-3	3-4	0-2	2-3	0-9	0-3		0-5	3-2	0-4	1-5	1-6	1-4
Gala Fairydean Rovers	0-0	2-0	1-5	2-7	0-3	3-4	1-2	1-2	1-4	1-6	2-0	2-1		4-1	1-1	1-6	0-2	2-0
Gretna 2008	0-4	0-1	1-2	1-0	0-1	3-3	2-1	2-3	1-4	0-7	1-4	2-1	0-0		0-3	2-9	1-3	1-1
Heart of Midlothian B	2-1	6-0	4-2	3-2	1-1	2-1	3-0	1-2	1-3	4-2	5-3	12ñ0	3-1	7-0		2-2	3-0	0-1
Linlithgow Rose	0-1	1-1	1-2	1-0	1-0	2-2	2-0	0-1	2-4	2-2	2-0	2-2	5-0	5-0	0-1		1-0	3-1
Tranent	1-1	0-1	1-2	0-0	1-1	1-0	0-1	1-0	2-2	0-3	3-4	6-2	2-1	8-0	0-1	2-1		2-1
University of Stirling	2-2	0-2	3-1	1-4	1-0	0-2	0-2	2-1	0-3	1-1	1-0	3-2	0-1	3-1	2-1	1-2	1-2	

Heart of Midlothian "B" vs Civil Service Strollers was abandoned after 77 minutes due to a medical emergency. The score at the time stood as the final result.

Scottish Lowland Football League
Season 2023/2024

East Kilbride	34	26	3	5	96	43	81
Heart of Midlothian "B"	34	21	6	7	92	43	69
Bo'ness United	34	21	4	9	72	50	67
Cumbernauld Colts	34	19	8	7	70	43	65
Tranent	34	18	6	10	69	42	60
Celtic "B"	34	18	5	11	80	47	59
Civil Service Strollers	34	17	5	12	51	48	56
Linlithgow Rose	34	14	8	12	63	43	50
Albion Rovers	34	12	10	12	43	36	46
Cowdenbeath	34	12	10	12	55	56	46
University of Stirling	34	13	7	14	50	53	46
Caledonian Braves	34	12	9	13	47	43	45
Berwick Rangers	34	12	6	16	42	48	42
East Stirlingshire	34	12	4	18	58	68	40
Broomhill	34	11	6	17	56	59	39
Gala Fairydean Rovers	34	9	5	20	45	87	32
Gretna 2008	34	3	3	28	26	114	12
Edinburgh University	**34**	**2**	**3**	**29**	**40**	**132**	**9**

Scottish Cup 2023/2024

Round	Date	Home	Score	Away	Score	
Round 1	23rd Sep 2023	Culter	3	Deveronvale	4	(aet)
Round 1	23rd Sep 2023	Penicuik Athletic	0	Pollok	6	
Round 1	23rd Sep 2023	Cowdenbeath	2	Linlithgow Rose	1	(aet)
Round 1	23rd Sep 2023	Clachnacuddin	1	Inverurie Loco Works	0	
Round 1	23rd Sep 2023	Dalkeith Thistle	0	Clydebank	7	
Round 1	23rd Sep 2023	Formartine United	3	Threave Rovers	2	
Round 1	23rd Sep 2023	Dunipace	1	Cumnock Juniors	3	(aet)
Round 1	23rd Sep 2023	Gala Fairydean Rovers	8	Strathspey Thistle	2	
Round 1	23rd Sep 2023	Lossiemouth	0	Beith Juniors	4	
Round 1	23rd Sep 2023	Wick Academy	1	Jeanfield Swifts	3	
Round 1	23rd Sep 2023	Edinburgh University	2	Dunbar United	3	
Round 1	23rd Sep 2023	Caledonian Braves	1	Fraserburgh	2	
Round 1	23rd Sep 2023	Banks O' Dee	6	Dalbeattie Star	0	
Round 1	23rd Sep 2023	Bo'ness United	3	Darvel	0	
Round 1	23rd Sep 2023	Turriff United	2	Sauchie Juniors	1	
Round 1	23rd Sep 2023	Golspie Sutherland	1	Forres Mechanics	1	(aet)
		Forres Mechanics won 8-7 on penalties.				
Round 1	23rd Sep 2023	Tayport	0	Buckie Thistle	4	
Round 1	23rd Sep 2023	Camelon Juniors	1	Civil Service Strollers	2	
Round 1	23rd Sep 2023	Brechin City	4	Rothes	0	
Round 1	23rd Sep 2023	East Stirlingshire	0	Huntly	1	
Round 1	23rd Sep 2023	Musselburgh Athletic	1	Gretna 2008	1	(aet)
		Musselburgh Athletic won 4-3 on penalties.				
Round 1	23rd Sep 2023	East Kilbride	8	Whitehill Welfare	0	
Round 1	23rd Sep 2023	Keith	2	Luncarty	5	
Round 1	23rd Sep 2023	Broxburn Athletic	2	Nairn County	1	
Round 1	23rd Sep 2023	Dundonald Bluebell	2	Kilwinning Rangers	3	
Round 1	23rd Sep 2023	Brora Rangers	5	Berwick Rangers	1	
Round 1	23rd Sep 2023	Tranent	4	Hutchison Vale	1	
Round 1	23rd Sep 2023	St Andrews United	1	Auchinleck Talbot	0	
Round 1	24th Sep 2023	Broomhill	3	Cumbernauld Colts	1	
Round 1	25th Sep 2023	University of Stirling	1	Albion Rovers	3	
Round 2	28th Oct 2023	Beith Juniors	1	Broomhill	3	
Round 2	28th Oct 2023	Civil Service Strollers	0	Stranraer	3	
Round 2	28th Oct 2023	Albion Rovers	2	St Andrews United	1	
Round 2	28th Oct 2023	Stenhousemuir	0	Brora Rangers	2	
Round 2	28th Oct 2023	Cumnock Juniors	2	Turriff United	1	
Round 2	28th Oct 2023	Kilwinning Rangers	0	Cowdenbeath	1	
Round 2	28th Oct 2023	Peterhead	3	Clachnacuddin	1	
Round 2	28th Oct 2023	Deveronvale	0	Broxburn Athletic	1	
Round 2	28th Oct 2023	Forres Mechanics	0	Buckie Thistle	1	
Round 2	28th Oct 2023	Dumbarton	3	Banks O' Dee	2	
Round 2	28th Oct 2023	Dunbar United	1	East Fife	0	
Round 2	28th Oct 2023	Fraserburgh	1	Bonnyrigg Rose	2	(aet)
Round 2	28th Oct 2023	Tranent	7	East Kilbride	0	
Round 2	28th Oct 2023	Formartine United	3	Clydebank	2	
Round 2	28th Oct 2023	Brechin City	1	The Spartans	2	
Round 2	28th Oct 2023	Jeanfield Swifts	6	Elgin City	0	
Round 2	28th Oct 2023	Huntly	1	Forfar Athletic	4	(aet)
Round 2	28th Oct 2023	Pollok	5	Gala Fairydean Rovers	2	
Round 2	30th Oct 2023	Musselburgh Athletic	2	Clyde	3	(aet)
Round 2	4th Nov 2023	Luncarty	0	Bo'ness United	1	

Round	Date	Home	Score	Away	Score	
Round 3	24th Nov 2023	Dunfermline Athletic	0	Raith Rovers	3	
Round 3	24th Nov 2023	Clyde	2	Jeanfield Swifts	0	
Round 3	25th Nov 2023	Cumnock Juniors	0	Broomhill	3	
Round 3	25th Nov 2023	Partick Thistle	3	Queen's Park	0	
Round 3	25th Nov 2023	Greenock Morton	4	Bo'ness United	0	
Round 3	25th Nov 2023	Annan Athletic	4	Dumbarton	5	(aet)
Round 3	25th Nov 2023	Stranraer	0	Airdrieonians	1	
Round 3	25th Nov 2023	Dunbar United	1	Alloa Athletic	2	
Round 3	25th Nov 2023	Broxburn Athletic	2	Buckie Thistle	2	(aet)
		Buckie Thistle won 5-4 on penalties.				
Round 3	25th Nov 2023	Hamilton Academical	0	Kelty Hearts	2	
Round 3	25th Nov 2023	Brora Rangers	1	Pollok	0	
Round 3	25th Nov 2023	Montrose	3	Edinburgh City	0	
Round 3	25th Nov 2023	Falkirk	3	Formartine United	0	
Round 3	25th Nov 2023	Stirling Albion	0	Cove Rangers	2	
Round 3	25th Nov 2023	Inverness Caledonian Thistle	2	Cowdenbeath	0	
Round 3	25th Nov 2023	Peterhead	1	Ayr United	2	
Round 3	25th Nov 2023	Tranent	0	Forfar Athletic	1	
Round 3	25th Nov 2023	Queen of the South	2	Dundee United	2	(aet)
		Queen of the South won 4-3 on penalties.				
Round 3	25th Nov 2023	The Spartans	2	Arbroath	1	
Round 3	25th Nov 2023	Albion Rovers	0	Bonnyrigg Rose	1	
Round 4	19th Jan 2024	Clyde	0	Aberdeen	2	
Round 4	20th Jan 2024	The Spartans	1	Heart of Midlothian	2	
Round 4	20th Jan 2024	Ayr United	3	Kelty Hearts	0	
Round 4	20th Jan 2024	Kilmarnock	2	Dundee	0	
Round 4	20th Jan 2024	Greenock Morton	2	Montrose	0	
Round 4	20th Jan 2024	Inverness Caledonian Thistle	4	Broomhill	0	
Round 4	20th Jan 2024	St Mirren	1	Queen of the South	0	
Round 4	20th Jan 2024	Bonnyrigg Rose	2	Falkirk	1	
Round 4	20th Jan 2024	Livingston	2	Raith Rovers	1	
Round 4	20th Jan 2024	Motherwell	3	Alloa Athletic	1	
Round 4	20th Jan 2024	Ross County	0	Partick Thistle	3	
Round 4	20th Jan 2024	Forfar Athletic	0	Hibernian	1	
Round 4	20th Jan 2024	Airdrieonians	1	St Johnstone	0	
Round 4	20th Jan 2024	Dumbarton	1	Rangers	4	
Round 4	21st Jan 2024	Celtic	5	Buckie Thistle	0	
Round 4	30th Jan 2024	Brora Rangers	1	Cove Rangers	3	(aet)
Round 5	9th Feb 2024	Greenock Morton	2	Motherwell	1	
Round 5	10th Feb 2024	Kilmarnock	2	Cove Rangers	0	
Round 5	10th Feb 2024	Inverness Caledonian Thistle	1	Hibernian	3	
Round 5	10th Feb 2024	Aberdeen	2	Bonnyrigg Rose	0	
Round 5	10th Feb 2024	Partick Thistle	2	Livingston	3	(aet)
Round 5	10th Feb 2024	Rangers	2	Ayr United	0	
Round 5	11th Feb 2024	St Mirren	0	Celtic	2	
Round 5	11th Feb 2024	Airdrieonians	1	Heart of Midlothian	4	
Quarter-final	9th Mar 2024	Aberdeen	3	Kilmarnock	1	
Quarter-final	10th Mar 2024	Celtic	4	Livingston	2	
Quarter-final	10th Mar 2024	Hibernian	0	Rangers	2	
Quarter-final	11th Mar 2024	Greenock Morton	0	Heart of Midlothian	1	

Semi-final	20th Apr 2024	Aberdeen	3	Celtic	3	(aet)
		Celtic won 6-5 on penalties.				
Semi-final	21th Apr 2024	Rangers	2	Heart of Midlothian	0	
FINAL	25th May 2024	Celtic	1	Rangers	0	

Scottish League Cup 2023/2024

Scottish League Cup 2023/2024 Season Group A	Ayr United	Stirling Albion	St. Johnstone	Stenhousemuir	Alloa Athletic
Ayr United	■		1-0	6-0	
Stirling Albion	1-1 (3-4p)	■		2-1	
St Johnstone	1-2	0-4	■		
Stenhousemuir			1-0	■	1-3
Alloa Athletic		1-2	0-4		■

Scottish League Cup 2023/2024 Season Group B	Partick Thistle	Falkirk	Dundee United	The Spartans	Peterhead
Partick Thistle	■	2-2 (6-7p)		2-1	
Falkirk		■	0-1		4-1
Dundee United	1-2		■		3-0
The Spartans		1-2	1-0	■	
Peterhead	1-1p		-	1-2	■

The top team in each group progressed to the Second Round and the three best runners-up between the 8 groups also progressed.

In the tables below, PW indicates a penalty shoot-out win and a bonus point, PL indicates a shoot-out loss.

Group A	Pld	W	PW	PL	L	GF	GA	Pts
Ayr United	4	3	1	0	0	10	2	11
Stirling Albion	4	3	0	1	0	9	3	10
St. Johnstone	4	1	0	0	3	5	7	3
Stenhousemuir	4	1	0	0	3	3	6	3
Alloa Athletic	4	1	0	0	3	4	13	3

Group B	Pld	W	PW	PL	L	GF	GA	Pts
Partick Thistle	4	2	1	1	0	7	5	9
Falkirk	4	2	1	0	1	8	5	8
Dundee United	4	2	0	0	2	5	3	6
The Spartans	4	2	0	0	2	5	5	6
Peterhead	4	0	0	1	3	3	10	1

Group C	Pld	W	PW	PL	L	GF	GA	Pts
Livingston	4	3	0	1	0	10	1	10
Hamilton Academical	4	2	1	1	0	7	4	9
Cove Rangers	4	2	1	0	1	10	11	8
Brechin City	4	1	0	0	3	4	8	3
Clyde	4	0	0	0	4	4	11	0

Group D	Pld	W	PW	PL	L	GF	GA	Pts
Ross County	4	3	0	1	0	13	6	10
Greenock Morton	4	3	0	0	1	11	4	9
Kelty Hearts	4	2	1	0	1	11	9	8
Stranraer	4	1	0	0	3	3	11	3
Edinburgh City	4	0	0	0	4	6	14	0

Scottish League Cup 2023/2024 Season Group C	Livingston	Hamilton Academical	Cove Rangers	Brechin City	Clyde
Livingston	■	1-1 (1-4p)		1-0	
Hamilton Academical		■	2-2 (2-4p)	1-0	
Cove Rangers	0-5		■		5-2
Brechin City	0-3		2-3	■	
Clyde		1-3		1-2	■

Scottish League Cup 2023/2024 Season Group D	Ross County	Greenock Morton	Kelty Hearts	Stranraer	Edinburgh City
Ross County	■	2-1	3-3 (3-4p)		
Greenock Morton		■		3-0	4-1
Kelty Hearts		1-3	■	2-0	
Stranraer	1-5			■	2-1
Edinburgh City	1-3		3-5		■

Scottish League Cup 2023/2024 Season Group E

	Airdrieonians	Dundee	Dumbarton	Inverness Caledonian Thistle	Bonnyrigg Rose
Airdrieonians		1-0	2-0		
Dundee			3-1	1-0	
Dumbarton				2-1	0-0 (4-3p)
Inverness Caledonian Thistle	2-3				2-1
Bonnyrigg Rose	0-1	0-1			

Scottish League Cup 2023/2024 Season Group F

	Kilmarnock	Raith Rovers	Dunfermline Athletic	Albion Rovers	Annan Athletic
Kilmarnock		2-2 (4-5p)			3-0
Raith Rovers			1-1 (2-4p)	2-0	
Dunfermline Athletic	0-2				4-0
Albion Rovers	1-2		0-3		
Annan Athletic		2-3		1-2	

In the tables below, PW indicates a penalty shoot-out win and a bonus point, PL indicates a shoot-out loss.

Group E	Pld	W	PW	PL	L	GF	GA	Pts
Airdrieonians	4	4	0	0	0	7	2	12
Dundee	4	3	0	0	1	5	2	9
Dumbarton	4	1	1	0	2	3	6	5
Inverness Caledonian Thistle	4	1	0	0	3	5	7	3
Bonnyrigg Rose	4	0	0	1	3	1	4	1

Group F	Pld	W	PW	PL	L	GF	GA	Pts
Kilmarnock	4	3	0	1	0	9	3	10
Raith Rovers	4	2	1	1	0	8	5	9
Dunfermline Athletic	4	2	1	0	1	8	3	8
Albion Rovers	4	1	0	0	3	3	8	3
Annan Athletic	4	0	0	0	4	3	12	0

Group G	Pld	W	PW	PL	L	GF	GA	Pts
Motherwell	4	3	1	0	0	9	3	11
Queen of the South	4	2	0	2	0	7	4	8
East Fife	4	1	2	0	1	3	4	7
Queen's Park	4	1	0	1	2	6	3	4
Elgin City	4	0	0	0	4	1	12	0

Group H	Pld	W	PW	PL	L	GF	GA	Pts
St Mirren	4	3	0	0	1	9	1	9
Forfar Athletic	4	3	0	0	1	6	6	9
Arbroath	4	1	1	0	2	5	8	5
Montrose	4	1	1	0	2	3	6	5
Cowdenbeath	4	0	0	2	2	2	4	2

Scottish League Cup 2022/2023 Season Group G

	Inverness Caledonian Thistle	Livingston	Cove Rangers	Albion Rovers	Kelty Hearts
Inverness Cal. Thistle		1-1 (5-3p)	4-0		
Livingston	1-2			2-0	
Cove Rangers		1-2			2-3
Albion Rovers		2-3	1-2		
Kelty Hearts	0-1			0-2	

Scottish League Cup 2022/2023 Season Group H

	Dundee	Hamilton Academical	Queen's Park	Forfar Athletic	Stranraer
Dundee		3-0		5-1	
Hamilton Academical			1-1 (5-3p)		5-2
Queen's Park	1-2			4-1	
Forfar Athletic		0-3			3-0
Stranraer	0-3		2-5		

The three runners-up with the best record progressed to the Second Round:

Best Runners-up	Pld	W	PW	PL	L	GF	GA	Pts
Stirling Albion	4	3	0	1	0	9	3	10
Greenock Morton	4	3	0	0	1	11	4	9
Raith Rovers	4	2	1	1	0	8	5	9
Hamilton Academical	4	2	1	1	0	7	4	9
Dundee	4	3	0	0	1	5	2	9
Forfar Athletic	4	3	0	0	1	6	6	9
Falkirk	4	2	1	0	1	8	5	8
Queen of the South	4	2	0	2	0	7	4	8

Round 2	18th Aug 2023	Stirling Albion	1	Aberdeen	2	
Round 2	19th Aug 2023	Rangers	2	Greenock Morton	1	
Round 2	19th Aug 2023	Airdrieonians	3	Ross County	4	(aet)
Round 2	19th Aug 2023	Livingston	2	Ayr United	0	
Round 2	19th Aug 2023	St Mirren	1	Motherwell	0	
Round 2	20th Aug 2023	Hibernian	2	Raith Rovers	1	
Round 2	20th Aug 2023	Heart of Midlothian	4	Partick Thistle	0	
Round 2	20th Aug 2023	Kilmarnock	1	Celtic	0	
Quarter-final	26th Sep 2023	Kilmarnock	1	Heart of Midlothian	2	
Quarter-final	27th Sep 2023	Hibernian	4	St Mirren	2	
Quarter-final	27th Sep 2023	Ross County	1	Aberdeen	2	
Quarter-final	27th Sep 2023	Rangers	4	Livingston	0	
Semi-final	4th Nov 2023	Hibernian	0	Aberdeen	1	
Semi-final	5th Nov 2023	Heart of Midlothian	1	Rangers	3	
FINAL	17th Dec 2023	Rangers	1	Aberdeen	0	

Scottish Challenge Cup 2023/2024

The competition included two guest teams from Northern Ireland, two teams from Wales, four teams each from the Highland Football League and Lowland Football League plus Under-21 teams from 11 of the 12 Scottish Premier League.

First Round – North Section						
Round 1	1st Aug 2023	Brechin City	2	Heart of Midlothian B	2	
		Brechin City won 5-3 on penalties				
Round 1	1st Aug 2023	Elgin City	2	St Johnstone B	0	
Round 1	2nd Aug 2023	Hibernian B	1	Formartine United	1	
		Hibernian B won 3-2 on penalties				
Round 1	2nd Aug 2023	Brora Rangers	1	Aberdeen B	1	
		Aberdeen B won 4-2 on penalties.				
Round 1	2nd Aug 2023	Dundee B	4	Buckie Thistle	0	
First Round – South Section						
Round 1	1st Aug 2023	St Mirren B	2	Albion Rovers	2	
		Albion Rovers won 4-2 on penalties				
Round 1	1st Aug 2023	Tranent	0	Motherwell B	0	
		Tranent won 3-1 on penalties.				
Round 1	1st Aug 2023	The Spartans	0	Rangers B	3	
Round 1	1st Aug 2023	Kilmarnock B	3	Bonnyrigg Rose	1	
Round 1	2nd Aug 2023	University of Stirling	4	Livingston B	0	
Round 1	2nd Aug 2023	Celtic B	1	East Kilbride	3	
Second Round – North Section						
Round 2	15th Aug 2023	Brechin City	0	Hibernian B	4	
Round 2	15th Aug 2023	Aberdeen B	3	Peterhead	5	
Round 2	15th Aug 2023	Dundee B	0	East Fife	0	
		East Fife won 5-3 on penalties				
Round 2	15th Aug 2023	Elgin City	0	Forfar Athletic	0	
		Elgin City won 4-3 on penalties				
Second Round – South Section						
Round 2	15th Aug 2023	Albion Rovers	2	Tranent	0	
Round 2	15th Aug 2023	Annan Athletic	3	Stranraer	1	
Round 2	15th Aug 2023	Stirling Albion	0	East Kilbride	3	
Round 2	15th Aug 2023	Stenhousemuir	1	Rangers B	2	
Round 2	16th Aug 2023	Clyde	1	University of Stirling	3	
Round 2	16th Aug 2023	Kilmarnock B	1	Dumbarton	1	
		Dumbarton won 9-8 on penalties.				
Round 3	5th Sep 2023	Ayr United	0	Falkirk	1	
Round 3	8th Sep 2023	Hibernian B	0	The New Saints	3	
Round 3	9th Sep 2023	East Fife	2	Albion Rovers	1	
Round 3	9th Sep 2023	Raith Rovers	3	Cliftonville	0	
Round 3	9th Sep 2023	Edinburgh City	1	East Kilbride	4	
Round 3	9th Sep 2023	Annan Athletic	0	Peterhead	2	
Round 3	9th Sep 2023	Cove Rangers	0	Montrose	2	
Round 3	9th Sep 2023	Dumbarton	1	Kelty Hearts	3	
Round 3	9th Sep 2023	University of Stirling	2	Airdrieonians	3	

Round 3	9th Sep 2023	Greenock Morton	2	Elgin City	1
Round 3	9th Sep 2023	Dundee United	3	Dunfermline Athletic	0
Round 3	9th Sep 2023	Arbroath	4	Inverness Caledonian Thistle	2
Round 3	9th Sep 2023	Partick Thistle	2	Queen of the South	3
Round 3	9th Sep 2023	Coleraine	1	Hamilton Academical	3
Round 3	9th Sep 2023	Bala Town	0	Queen's Park	3
Round 3	26 Sep 2023	Rangers B	4	Alloa Athletic	1
Round 4	14th Oct 2023	Raith Rovers	3	Montrose	1
Round 4	14th Oct 2023	East Kilbride	2	Hamilton Academical	5
Round 4	14th Oct 2023	Falkirk	1	Queen's Park	0
Round 4	14th Oct 2023	Queen of the South	1	Arbroath	2
Round 4	14th Oct 2023	Greenock Morton	4	Kelty Hearts	1
Round 4	14th Oct 2023	The New Saints	2	East Fife	2
		The New Saints won 5-4 on penalties			
Round 4	14th Oct 2023	Peterhead	0	Dundee United	2
Round 4	7th Nov 2023	Rangers B	2	Airdrieonians	4
Quarter-final	17th Nov 2023	Falkirk	4	Dundee United	2
Quarter-final	17th Nov 2023	Hamilton Academical	1	Raith Rovers	4
Quarter-final	18th Nov 2023	The New Saints	4	Arbroath	1
Quarter-final	18th Nov 2023	Greenock Morton	0	Airdrieonians	0
		Airdrieonians won 6 5 on penalties.			
Semi-final	2nd Feb 2024	Raith Rovers	1	Airdrieonians	0
Semi-final	3rd Feb 2024	Falkirk	0	The New Saints	1
FINAL	24th Mar 2024	The New Saints	1	Airdrieonians	2

SCOTLAND INTERNATIONAL LINE-UPS & STATISTICS 2023

8th September 2023
v CYPRUS (ECQ) Larnaca
A. Gunn	Norwich City
A. Hickey	Brentford (sub. N. Patterson 84)
A. Robertson	Liverpool
S. McTominay	Man. United (sub. R. Christie 90)
K. Tierney	Real Sociedad
J. McGinn	Aston Villa (sub. S. Armstrong 84)
C. McGregor	Celtic
C. Adams	Southampton (sub. L. Dykes 67)
J. Hendry	Al-Ettifaq
B. Gilmour	Brighton & H.A. (sub. K. McLean 67)
R. Porteous	Watford

Result 3-0 McTominay, Porteous, McGinn

12th September 2023
v ENGLAND Hampden Park
A. Gunn	Norwich City
A. Hickey	Brentford (sub. N. Patterson 89)
A. Robertson	Liverpool
S. McTominay	Manchester United
K. Tierney	Real Sociedad (sub. S. Armstrong 82)
J. McGinn	Aston Villa (sub. L. Ferguson 82)
C. McGregor	Celtic (sub. R. Jack 89)
C. Adams	Southampton (sub. R. Christie 59)
J. Hendry	Al-Ettifaq
B. Gilmour	Brighton & H.A. (sub. L. Dykes 60)
R. Porteous	Watford

Result 1-3 Maguire (o.g.)

12th October 2023
v SPAIN (ECQ) Seville
A. Gunn	Norwich City
A. Hickey	Brentford
A. Robertson	Liverpool (sub. N. Patterson 44)
S. McTominay	Manchester United
J. McGinn	Aston Villa
C. McGregor	Celtic (sub. K. McLean 87)
L. Dykes	Q.P.R. (sub. C. Adams 79)
R. Christie	Bournemouth (sub. S. Armstrong 79)
J. Hendry	Al-Ettifaq
R. Porteous	Watford (sub. B. Gilmour 87)
S. McKenna	Nottingham Forest

Result 0-2

17th October 2023
v FRANCE Lille
L. Kelly (sub. Z. Clark 45)	
S. McTominay	Manchester United
L. Cooper	Leeds United
C. Adams	Southampton (sub. J. Brown 64)
J. Hendry	Al-Ettifaq
B. Gilmour	Brighton & H.A. (sub. S. Armstrong '76)
S. McKenna	Nottingham Forest
L. Ferguson	Bologna
G. Taylor	Celtic
N. Patterson	Hearts (sub. J. McGinn 89)
K. McLean	Norwich City (sub. R. Christie 76)

Result 1-4 Gilmour

16th November 2023
v GEORGIA (ECQ) Tbilisi
Z. Clark	Heart of Midlothian
G. Taylor	Celtic (sub. S. Armstrong 79)
S. McTominay	Manchester United
J. McGinn	Aston Villa
C. McGregor	Celtic
L. Dykes	Q.P.R. (sub. L. Shankland 86)
R. Christie	Bournemouth (sub. L. Ferguson 46)
B. Gilmour	Brighton & H.A. (sub. K. McLean 46)
R. Porteous	Watford
S. McKenna	Nottingham Forest
N. Patterson	Hearts (A. Ralston 79)

Result 2-2 McTominay, Shankland

19th November 2023
v NORWAY (ECQ) Hampden Park
Z. Clark	Heart of Midlothian
G. Taylor	Celtic
S. McTominay	Manchester United
J. McGinn	Aston Villa (sub. R. Jack 79)
C. McGregor	Celtic (sub. L. Shankland 89)
J. Hendry	Al-Ettifaq
S. McKenna	Nottingham Forest
S. Armstrong	Southampton (sub. R. Christie 70)
J. Brown	Luton Town (sub. L. Dykes 70)
N. Patterson	Heart of Midlothian
K. McLean	Norwich City (sub. L. Ferguson 70)

Result 3-3 McGinn, Ostigard (o.g.), Armstrong

SCOTLAND INTERNATIONAL LINE-UPS & STATISTICS 2024

22nd March 2024
v NETHERLANDS *Amsterdam*
A. Gunn — Norwich City
A. Robertson — Liverpool
S. McTominay — Manchester United
K. Tierney — Real Sociedad (sub. J. Souttar 68)
J. McGinn — Aston Villa (sub. K. McLean 85)
R. Christie — Bournemouth (sub. S. Armstrong 74)
J. Hendry — Al-Ettifaq
B. Gilmour — Brighton & H.A. (sub. L. Ferguson 69)
R. Porteous — Watford
L. Shankland — Hearts (sub. C. Adams 68)
N. Patterson — Everton
Result 0-4

26th March 2024
v NORTHERN IRELAND *Hampden Park*
A. Gunn — Norwich City
A. Robertson — Liverpool (sub. L. Ferguson 37)
S. McTominay — Manchester United
L. Cooper — Leeds United
K. Tierney — Real Sociedad
J. McGinn — Aston Villa (sub. S. Armstrong 78)
L. Dykes — Q.P.R. (sub. C. Adams 70)
R. Christie — Bournemouth (sub. L. Shankland 78)
J. Hendry — Al-Ettifaq
B. Gilmour — Brighton & H.A. (sub. K. McLean 70)
N. Patterson — Everton
Result 0-1

3rd June 2024
v GIBRALTAR *Gibraltar*
Z. Clark — Heart of Midlothian
A. Robertson — Liverpool (sub. K. Tierney 66)
G. Hanley — Norwich City (sub. L. Cooper 46)
J. McGinn — Aston Villa
R. Christie — Bournemouth
B. Gilmour — Brighton & H.A. (sub. R. Jack 73)
R. Porteous — Watford
L. Shankland — Heart of Midlothian
R. McCrorie — Bristol City
K. McLean — Norwich City (sub. C. McGregor 73)
J. Forrest — Celtic (sub. C. Adams 66)
Result 2-0 Christie, Adams

7th June 2024
v FINLAND *Hampden Park*
A. Gunn — Norwich City (sub. C. Gordon 69)
A. Ralston — Celtic
A. Robertson — Liverpool (sub. G. Taylor 63)
G. Hanley — Norwich City (sub. S. McKenna 79)
K. Tierney — Real Sociedad
J. McGinn — Aston Villa
C. McGregor — Celtic
L. Shankland — Hearts (sub. T. Conway 63)
R. Christie — Bournemouth (sub. L. Morgan 79)
J. Hendry — Al-Ettifaq
B. Gilmour — Brighton & H.A. (sub. R. Jack 69)
Result 2-2 Hoskonen (o.g.), Shankland

14th June 2024
v GERMANY (EC) *Munich*
A. Gunn — Norwich City
A. Ralston — Celtic
A. Robertson — Liverpool
S. McTominay — Manchester United
K. Tierney — Real Sociedad (sub. S. McKenna 77)
J. McGinn — Aston Villa (sub. K. McLean 67)
C. McGregor — Celtic (sub. B. Gilmour 67)
C. Adams — Southampton (sub. G. Hanley 46)
R. Christie — Bournemouth (sub. L. Shankland 82)
J. Hendry — Al-Ettifaq
R. Porteous — Watford
Result 1-5 Ruediger (o.g.)

19th June 2024
v SWITZERLAND (EC) *Cologne*
A. Gunn — Norwich City
A. Ralston — Celtic
A. Robertson — Liverpool
S. McTominay — Manchester United
G. Hanley — Norwich City
K. Tierney — Real Sociedad (sub. S. McKenna 61)
J. McGinn — Aston Villa (sub. R. Christie 90)
C. McGregor — Celtic
C. Adams — Southampton (sub. L. Shankland 90)
J. Hendry — Al-Ettifaq
B. Gilmour — Brighton & H.A. (sub. K. McLean 79)
Result 1-1 McTominay

SCOTLAND INTERNATIONAL LINE-UPS AND STATISTICS 2024

23rd June 2024
v HUNGARY (EC) *Stuttgart*
A. Gunn   Norwich City
A. Ralston   Celtic (sub. K. McLean 83)
A. Robertson   Liverpool (sub. L. Morgan 89)
S. McTominay   Manchester United
G. Hanley   Norwich City
J. McGinn   Aston Villa (sub. S. Armstrong 76)
C. McGregor   Celtic
C. Adams   Southampton (sub. L. Shankland 76)
J. Hendry   Al-Ettifaq
B. Gilmour   Brighton & H.A. (sub. R. Christie 83)
S. McKenna   Copenhagen

Result 0-1